The Classic Air Fryer Cookbook for UK

Fry, Bake, Roast the Traditional British Recipes with Air Fryer for Beginners, Colour Printed
Cookbook with Pictures and Cooking Timetable

Jade Howarth

Legal & Disclaimer

The content and information in this book is consistent and truthful, and it has been provided for informational, educational and business purposes only.

The illustrations in the book are from the website shutterstock.com, depositphoto.com and freepik.com and have been authorized.

The content and information contained in this book has been compiled from reliable sources, which are accurate based on the knowledge, belief, expertise and information of the Author. The author cannot be held liable for any omissions and/or errors.

Contributors:
Editor: Diana Zanen
Proofread: David Johnson
Cover Designer: Len Cheng
Typography Designer: Jonathan Stevens

CONTENT

Chapter 5 Fish and Seafood   26

Chapter 6 Meats   32

Chapter 7 Poultry   40

Chapter 8 Starters and Snacks — 46

Chapter 9 Desserts — 53

Conclusion — 60

Introduction

Cooking nicely done scotch eggs and sausages for breakfast has become easier than ever; with an Air fryer resting on your countertop, you cannot only create a complete English breakfast to start the day, but it has also made cooking shepherd's pies, roasted beef, steaks, all sorts of snacks and dessert possible. That's right; all your favourite English recipes can now be cooked using an air fryer in just a few minutes. The air fryer has a clear edge over all other cooking appliances when it comes to producing healthy, oil-free meals in great varieties. And through my extensive air fryer recipe collection for types of meal courses, I will show how exactly you can use the same air frying technology to create a variety of dishes for your dinner table. The menu in this cookbook has all the traditional English recipes like Beef Wellington, Bangers and Mash, and Welsh Rarebit, and they all are prepared using an Air fryer. So, go ahead, check out their ingredients and easy-to-follow instructions, then give them a try. Since air fryers are available in different models, and sizes and with different cooking modes, make sure to go through the user manual of your own air fryer before trying out any recipe from this cookbook- knowing your appliance really helps to get the best results.

Chapter 1 Understand the Air Fryer Basics

Speaking of understanding your appliance better, let me first explain what an air fryer is and how it really works. Air fryers were patented in 2005, although the technology used in them was tried and tested even before 2005. They were developed as a replacement for deep frying to avoid the fat and calories associated with cooking meals in hot oil. When the hot air touches the food, it creates a crispier texture on the outside and cooks the food from the inside. A light layer of oil is also sprayed over the food to preserve the moisture content.

How Does an Air Fryer Work?

A countertop appliance we all know as the "air fryer" essentially functions as a small convection oven. It uses heat and airflow from an internal fan instead of a lot of oil or fat to crisp up your French fries and cook your chicken wings evenly. The fan and heat are both present above the food being cooked in the fryer, which is holding it in a slotted basket. The Maillard reaction is used in deep fryers to cook crispy food. The Maillard reaction is a chemical process between amino acids that gives food a crispy texture and darkens its colour. It is actually named after Louis-Camille Maillard- A French chemist. By cooking your food with a thin coating of oil and circulating hot air, air fryers can mimic the Maillard process by simultaneously heating the food and causing the Maillard reaction. When compared to a deep fryer, air fryers can "cook" things like fries, chips, meat, breaded meals, and vegetables while using almost minimal oil since they can produce the Maillard reaction. The oil used for air frying is almost less than a tablespoon, or even less.

What to Cook in an Air Fryer?

The possibilities are endless with this little appliance. Some things, like fried chicken or breaded cauliflower florets, can be readily cooked in an air fryer. If they fit in your basket, air fryers can "cook" frozen delicacies like mozzarella sticks and personal pizzas to melty, cheesy, crunchy perfection. They can, among other things, bake bread, rotisserie, a chicken (if you have the attachment), roast vegetables, bake cakes and brownies, fry bacon, and make bread. The majority of fryers also have a useful recipe booklet.

Once you learn how they operate, they can be used to cook a variety of fresh items, including chicken, steak, pork chops, fish, and vegetables, as well as to thaw frozen goods. Because most meats are already so juicy, they don't need additional oil; simply season them with salt and your preferred herbs and spices. Always use dry seasonings since fewer moisture yields crispier results. Wait until the last few minutes of air frying to baste meats with barbecue sauce or honey.

Foods with little to no fat or lean cuts of meat need oil to be brown and crispy. Before seasoning, lightly oil boneless chicken breasts and pork chops. Due to their higher smoke points, vegetable or canola oil is typically advised since they can withstand the high heat in an air fryer.

In addition, vegetables must be coated in oil before air frying. Before air frying, we advise sprinkling them with salt but use a bit less than usual. Broccoli florets, Brussels sprouts, and baby potato halves all taste delicious when air-fried. They turn out so crunchy! Beets, butternut squash, and sweet potatoes all seem to get sweeter over time as they cook, while green beans and peppers cook quickly.

Benefits of an Air Fryer

An air fryer's benefits mainly include the ability to cook food quickly and crisply with little to no oil. Without any flavour loss, cutting the oil significantly reduces the amount of fat and calories. There are additional benefits of air fryers as well, such as:

* **Lesser Use of Oil**

You use a lot less oil while air frying than you use when you are deep frying or even pan frying and sautéing, which will save you money at the grocery store. Additionally, you won't have to stress about getting rid of a lot of oil, which might block your drainage system. Air frying decreases your food's calories and fat significantly in comparison to frying or sautéing. Comparing air fryers to deep fryers, the oil used can be reduced by up to 90%.

If you pan-fry your food, you would still require up to a cup of oil, and your food would be submerged in many cups of oil. Many foods can be prepared without using any oil. Many recipes that call for no additional oil at all in the air fryer are perfect for baking and desserts.

* **Reduced Cooking Time**

It only takes 30 minutes to cook chicken drumsticks in an air fryer set to 190 degrees. You would need to bake the same items for an hour at 180 degrees Celsius in a standard oven, rotating them halfway through. So, using an air fryer can help you save up to 50% of the time required to cook the same foods in an oven. Not even the time required to preheat your oven is included in that. Use as little as 1 tablespoon of oil while frying food. The majority of air fryer fried recipes ask for just 1 tablespoon of oil or a few sprays of spray oil.

* **Reduce Intake of Fat**

Using an air fryer does allow you to reduce your intake of fat and calories, provided that you were deep-frying or pan-frying before that. The food you might have been baking, boiling, braising, or sautéing before might not be considered healthier if you weren't doing a lot of frying before. But you'll find that the air fryer is healthier if you want to reduce your intake of calories, fat, and deep-fried food.

* **Do Not Release Heat into the Environment**

Even the most well-insulated home can still become hot during the summer when the oven is turned up for dinner. The air fryer, in contrast, produces no ambient heat at all. When it is cooking, the appliance itself only feels warm to the touch on the outside.

An Air Fryer doesn't produce a deep-fried stench that fills the kitchen. Deep fryers use high heat for cooking food, and because they are frequently open on top and produce a lot of heat and scents, your entire house may smell like fried food after a brief fry. That scent might be a lot worse if you fry up some fish tacos.

* **Splatter-Free Cooking**

Not only is the air fryer exceedingly simple to clean, but it also creates almost little mess at all. Since the food is entirely contained inside the basket, there won't be any splatter, oily residue, or other mess on the air fryer's exterior or on the tabletop.

Things to Consider Before Buying Your Air Fryer

The air fryer is undoubtedly the most sought-after kitchen appliance these days. I personally like to use an air fryer because of all the convenience it has brought to my life; I can practically "air fry or bake" anything without having to set up a deep-oil frying station or make a mess. Since there are so many air fryer brands, models, and sizes out there in the market, it is quite imperative to consider a few important factors about an air fry before buying a new one. I personally looked into these factors before buying my own air fryer:

- **Cooking Capacity**

There are several different sizes of air fryers in the market. In the UK, manufacturers frequently specify the capacity in litres. The smallest air fryer size you will likely find is 1.5 to 2 L; medium air fryers typically have a capacity of 3 to 5 L; and big air fryers can hold up to 12 L. Although I would say that when cooking for 1-2 people, cooking larger amounts and reserving one portion is a terrific method to batch cook without becoming tired. Cooking for one person may absolutely be done with the smallest size. A medium capacity would be advantageous for a family of four, while larger families undoubtedly require a larger one. You should also consider whether you want more than one drawer to have the space you require. Some manufacturers are releasing dual drawer models, which can be helpful if you want to simultaneously cook protein and starch, such as fish and chips, but at separate temperatures.

- **Functionality**

All air fry comes with the air frying option, but they are several models which also offer options like a rotisserie, dehydrator, grill, roast, reheat, and bake. The prices of multifunctional air fryers are much than the basic ones, so buy the model that suits your budget.

- **Shape and Width of Basket**

Besides the size, the shape and width of the air fryer basket also matter. For instance, if the basket has lesser width and great depth, you can fit a muffin tray or baking pan in it. I've tried a few different air fryer brands, but I particularly prefer air fryers with baskets wide enough to accommodate the gratin dishes and brownie pans.

- **Price**

Any appliance you buy will require you to take this into account. I personally believe it is worthwhile to spend on quality in terms of how the air fryer is constructed, but not necessarily in lots of functionality. I prefer to use minimal functionality, but the air fryer needs to be durable, as I use it more than once per day. Some air fryers are fancier on the outside, but they might not be that durable and effective, so invest in the ones which are good at air frying, not in the looks.

The best advice is generally to consider how you will use an air fryer, how many people you will be cooking for, whether it would fit in your kitchen, and whether it could stay out for use most of the time. Don't be fooled by any company's reputation; check the specification of each model, check which features are most suitable for you and then make your decision.

Cooking with an Air Fryer

If you are using the air fryer for the first time, then take apart all removable parts after you have opened the box. The parts of an air fryer usually include a detachable basket with a grate or perforated tray in the bottom. Clean and dry them first. Place the air fryer at least eight inches away from a wall on a heat-resistant surface. Reinstall the basket and grate.

1. Remember to Preheat

Similar to an oven, air fryers require preheating before adding food. This makes sure that your food starts cooking straight away, whether it's frozen fries or Air-Fryer Chocolate Chip Oatmeal Cookies. These appliances are rather small, so it usually just takes a few minutes for them to reach the desired temperature. If you are cooking meals in continuous sessions, then you don't have to preheat the air fryer every time.

2. Use Oil Mist

You might find that your favourite frozen fries or air-fryer appetisers appear a little paler after cooking. Recipes for air fryers won't necessarily turn the desired golden colour without oil. To consistently produce golden air-fried food without using too much oil, such as for delectable Air-Fryer Potato Chips, use a light mist of oil spray.

3. Don't Stuff the Basket Too Full

Only when there is enough room inside the air fryer basket for the air to flow can items that are air-fried come out to be crispy and golden. Foods should be cooked in a single layer for best results. This is crucial when cooking crusted chicken, air-fried hamburgers, and other dishes. The only exception would be a few veggie air fryer recipes. One pound of Brussels sprouts can be placed in the basket, and they can be roasted for 12- 15 minutes at 180 degrees Celsius while being stirred once.

4. Shake It or Flip the Food

Always flip, rotate, or shake the food in the air fryer basket to help it crisp (much like rotating chicken tenders, fish fillets, or fries midway through cooking in a conventional oven). This step allows the food to be cooked evenly.

5. Leave the Trays and Baskets Un-greased.

It's so simple to air fry that you may even skip greasing the tray and the basket within. Besides a light spray to aid in browning, air-fryer dishes like Air-Fryer Ravioli and frozen items can be cooked without any added grease.

6. When Cooking Beef, Use a Thermometer.

Checking the temperature using a meat thermometer is a crucial step for safety because the food might brown nicely on the outside before reaching an optimum temperature on the inside. That holds true for both fresh and frozen meat cooked in an air fryer.

7. Reheat Leftovers in the Air Fryer.

While you can cook a lot of meals and appetisers from scratch with your air fryer, you can also use it to reheat your food from the day before. The air fryer gives anything, including leftover pizza and day-old fried chicken, a new lease on life. The meal is heated uniformly and is given the crisp texture that microwaved leftovers do not have. How to reheat leftover fries and other foods in your air fryer is shown here.

8. While in Use, Give the Appliance Some Room.

Be careful to keep your air fryer at least 6 inches away from any neighbouring walls when using it. This will improve the air fryer's ability to draw in air for circulation. You may store your air fryer in a cabinet or at the back of your counter once you're done using it, and it has cooled.

How to Clean the Air Fryer

After each cooking session, thoroughly clean your air fryer by shaking off any extra crumbs and quickly washing any components that have direct contact with food. If you follow these instructions each time you use your air fryer, extensive cleaning won't be needed every now and then. The fan and heating coils inside the air fryer eventually collect some grease buildup, much like a traditional oven does, so even if you have the best air fryer, it still needs cleaning. Here are a few simple steps to regularly clean your air fryer:

Step 1: To avoid unintentional burns, wait at least 10 minutes before attempting to clean a hot air fryer. After you are done cooking, leave the door or basket of your air fryer open to speed up the process. While you wait, concentrate on cleaning the remainder of your kitchen.

Step 2: Crumbs are a problem with the basket-style air fryers; you will need to clean them out frequently since little bits of food can get stuck underneath the basket and burn. Empty the basket chamber into the trash after removing it. Remember: Larger food bits belong in the trash container, while little crumbs can go down the garbage disposal.

Use a brush to remove any stray crumbs that stick to the door or hinges of a toaster oven-style air fryer by pulling out the crumb-catching tray on the bottom and shaking it off over the sink or trash can.

Step 3: You can wash the air fryer basket with soap and warm water, just like any other dish, so don't worry about not knowing how to do it. If you don't feel like cleaning it by hand and we don't blame you for that. To make cleaning simple, she explains that the majority of removable baskets may be placed on the top rack of the dishwasher.

Did food stick to the pan or basket? The pieces should be soaked in hot, soapy water for 20 to 30 minutes before being placed in the dishwasher. After that, scrape the softened gunk away with a brush.

Step 4: You can clean the inside of the air fryer after removing the basket, tray, and pan. Simply wipe the interior with a dry kitchen sponge that has been dampened with a little dish soap.

Deep Cleaning

When the performance of your air fryer starts to suffer, it's time for a deep clean. A thorough cleaning can improve the flavour of your air-fried meals and even increase the appliance's lifespan if your food isn't frying as quickly, isn't as crispy, or isn't cooking evenly.

First, unplug the device. Security first! Make sure your air fryer is unplugged before you start, as is the case with cleaning other small appliances. Since air frying uses relatively little oil, there won't be much greasy residue left behind after each usage, reducing the need for frequent cleaning of the air fryer's exterior. After every few sessions, clean the exterior with a moist cloth.

Apply a simple-to-make baking soda paste to any food particles or grease patches that have baked onto the interior of the air fryer: Several teaspoons of water and a half cup of baking soda should be combined. Scrub the inside of the air fryer thoroughly with a soft toothbrush or nonabrasive scrub brush. Never remove caked-on food or crumbs from the appliance with metal tools. They may erode the nonstick finish and render your air fryer inoperable.

After cleaning the air fryer's interior, give it a thorough wipe-down with a damp towel. Place the freshly cleaned basket, tray, or pan back after drying the equipment. And with that, you can use it again.

FAQs

1. What is the usual cooking capacity of an air fryer?

Depending on the type of food, most conventional air fryers can fit enough food for 2-4 servings. It's crucial to avoid stuffing the basket too full. If you decide to prepare an air frying recipe in multiple batches, begin monitoring the second batch for doneness a few minutes earlier because the air fryer would be already hot, and it will cook the second batch more quickly. The cooking capacity of all the different models varies, starting from 2-3L to up to 4-5L.

2. Do I need any more attachments or accessories for my air fryer?

A few air fryers come with extras like racks and pans. Even while these can be useful for specific tasks, most of the recipes from my collection require the normal air-fryer basket.

3. How can I stop food from sticking to the inside of the air fryer basket?

We advise lightly misting the basket with vegetable oil spray before adding dishes that are prone to sticking, like breaded chicken or delicate fish. Additionally, cleanup and the removal of some meals, particularly fish, can be made easy by lining the air fryer basket with a foil sheet before cooking.

4. What can I do if I smell smoke during air frying or if the smell coming from my air fryer changes?

Keep your air fryer clean! I have discovered that a dirty air fryer is the main cause of smoking and odour issues. Be careful to clean the area around the air fryer's heating element to get rid of any accumulated residue if you notice a lot of smoke or smell of burning even though your food hasn't really burned. Check periodically for food splatter and clean it with a mild detergent while it's cool.

Chapter 2 Breakfast

Bangers and Mash

Prep time: <5 minutes | Cook time: 10 minutes | Serves 8

cooking spray
590 ml beef stock
1 tbsp. plain flour
25 g butter
1 tbsp. cooking oil

1 medium onion, thinly sliced
6 large potatoes
8 sausages

1. Preheat the air fryer to 200ºC.
2. Peel the potatoes and boil them. Now for the gravy. Heat a large sauce pan with ½ tbsp. of cooking oil. Add in the sliced onions and allow them to sauté until they are browned.
3. Next add in the plain flour and use this to coat the onions.
4. Gradually add the stock at this stage and allow it to come to the boil. Simmer gently for 5-10 minutes,
5. Meanwhile, add the sausages in the air fryer basket and air fry for 3 minutes per side until they are browned all over and cooked thoroughly.
6. Once the potatoes are boiled, mash them with the butter plus a little salt and pepper.
7. Spoon mash potatoes on plate, place sausages on top of potatoes and finally spoon over the gravy.

Grit and Ham Fritters

Prep time: 15 minutes | Cook time: 20 minutes | Serves 6 to 8

960 ml water
260 g quick-cooking grits
¼ tsp. salt
2 tbsps. butter
470 g grated Cheddar cheese, divided
150 g finely diced ham

1 tbsp. chopped chives
Salt and freshly ground black pepper, to taste
1 egg, beaten
240 g panko bread crumbs
Cooking spray

1. Bring the water to a boil in a saucepan. Whisk in the grits and ¼ tsp. of salt, and cook for 7 minutes until the grits are soft. Remove the pan from the heat and stir in the butter and 80 g of the grated Cheddar cheese. Transfer the grits to a bowl and let them cool for 10 to 15 minutes.
2. Stir the ham, chives and the rest of the cheese into the grits and season with salt and pepper to taste.

Add the beaten egg and refrigerate the mixture for 30 minutes.
3. Put the panko bread crumbs in a shallow dish. Measure out ¼-cup portions of the grits mixture and shape them into patties. Coat all sides of the patties with the panko bread crumbs, patting them with the hands so the crumbs adhere to the patties. You should have about 16 patties. Spritz both sides of the patties with cooking spray.
4. Preheat the air fryer to 205ºC.
5. In batches of 5 or 6, air fry the fritters for 8 minutes. Using a flat spatula, flip the fritters over and air fry for another 4 minutes.
6. Serve hot.

Nut and Seed Muffins

Prep time: 15 minutes | Cook time: 10 minutes | Makes 8 muffins

60 g whole-wheat flour, plus 2 tbsps.
20 g oat bran
2 tbsps. flaxseed meal
55 g brown sugar
½ tsp. baking soda
½ tsp. baking powder
¼ tsp. salt
½ tsp. cinnamon
120 ml buttermilk
2 tbsps. melted butter

1 egg
½ tsp. pure vanilla extract
85 g grated carrots
40 g chopped pecans
40 g chopped walnuts
1 tbsp. pumpkin seeds
1 tbsp. sunflower seeds
Cooking spray
Special Equipment:
16 foil muffin cups, paper liners removed

1. Preheat the air fryer to 165ºC.
2. In a large bowl, stir together the flour, bran, flaxseed meal, sugar, baking soda, baking powder, salt, and cinnamon.
3. In a medium bowl, beat together the buttermilk, butter, egg, and vanilla. Pour into flour mixture and stir just until dry ingredients moisten. Do not beat.
4. Gently stir in carrots, nuts, and seeds.
5. Double up the foil cups so you have 8 total and spritz with cooking spray.
6. Put 4 foil cups in air fryer basket and divide half the batter among them.
7. Bake for 10 minutes or until a toothpick inserted in centre comes out clean.
8. Repeat step 7 to bake remaining 4 muffins.
9. Serve warm.

Ham and Corn Muffins

Prep time: 10 minutes | Cook time: 6 minutes | Makes 8 muffins

120 g yellow cornmeal	2 tbsps. rapeseed oil
30 g flour	120 ml milk
1½ tsps. baking powder	120 g shredded sharp
¼ tsp. salt	Cheddar cheese
1 egg, beaten	75 g diced ham

1. Preheat the air fryer to 200ºC.
2. In a medium bowl, stir together the cornmeal, flour, baking powder, and salt.
3. Add the egg, oil, and milk to dry ingredients and mix well.
4. Stir in shredded cheese and diced ham.
5. Divide batter among 8 parchment-paper-lined muffin cups.
6. Put 4 filled muffin cups in air fryer basket and bake for 5 minutes.
7. Reduce temperature to 165ºC and bake for 1 minute or until a toothpick inserted in centre of the muffin comes out clean.
8. Repeat steps 6 and 7 to bake remaining muffins.
9. Serve warm.

Quick Blueberry Muffins

Prep time: 10 minutes | Cook time: 12 minutes | Makes 8 muffins

162 g flour	1 egg
100 g sugar	120 ml milk
2 tsps. baking powder	130 g blueberries, fresh
¼ tsp. salt	or frozen and thawed
80 g rapeseed oil	

1. Preheat the air fryer to 170ºC.
2. In a medium bowl, stir together flour, sugar, baking powder, and salt.
3. In a separate bowl, combine oil, egg, and milk and mix well.
4. Add egg mixture to dry ingredients and stir just until moistened.
5. Gently stir in the blueberries.
6. Spoon batter evenly into parchment-paper-lined muffin cups.
7. Put 4 muffin cups in air fryer basket and bake for 12 minutes or until tops spring back when touched lightly.
8. Repeat previous step to bake remaining muffins.
9. Serve immediately.

Cheesy Chili Toast

Prep time: 5 minutes | Cook time: 5 minutes | Serves 1

2 tbsps. grated Parmesan cheese	room temperature
2 tbsps. grated Mozzarella cheese	10 to 15 thin slices serrano chili or jalapeño
2 tsps. salted butter, at	2 slices sourdough bread
	½ tsp. black pepper

1. Preheat the air fryer to 160ºC.
2. In a small bowl, stir together the Parmesan, Mozzarella, butter, and chilies.
3. Spread half the mixture onto one side of each slice of bread. Sprinkle with the pepper. Place the slices, cheese-side up, in the air fryer basket. Bake for 5 minutes, or until the cheese has melted and started to brown slightly.
4. Serve immediately.

All-in-One Toast

Prep time: 10 minutes | Cook time: 10 minutes | Serves 1

1 strip bacon, diced	Salt and freshly ground
1 slice 2-cm thick bread	black pepper, to taste
1 egg	55 g grated Colby cheese

1. Preheat the air fryer to 205ºC.
2. Air fry the bacon for 3 minutes, shaking the basket once or twice while it cooks. Remove the bacon to a paper towel lined plate and set aside.
3. Use a sharp paring knife to score a large circle in the middle of the slice of bread, cutting halfway through, but not all the way through to the cutting board. Press down on the circle in the centre of the bread slice to create an indentation.
4. Transfer the slice of bread, hole side up, to the air fryer basket. Crack the egg into the centre of the bread, and season with salt and pepper.
5. Adjust the air fryer temperature to 195ºC and air fry for 5 minutes. Sprinkle the grated cheese around the edges of the bread, leaving the centre of the yolk uncovered, and top with the cooked bacon. Press the cheese and bacon into the bread lightly to help anchor it to the bread and prevent it from blowing around in the air fryer.
6. Air fry for one or two more minutes, just to melt the cheese and finish cooking the egg. Serve immediately.

Scotch Egg

Prep time: 10 minutes | Cook time: 35 minutes | Serves 4

455 g sausage meat
1 tsp. dried onion powder
1 tsp. salt
4 hard-cooked eggs, peeled

80 g plain flour
80 g panko bread crumbs
1 egg, beaten

1. Preheat the air fryer to 200ºC.
2. In large bowl, mix pork sausage, onion and salt. Shape mixture into 4 equal burgers
3. Roll each hard-cooked egg in flour to coat; place on sausage burger and shape sausage around egg.
4. Dip each into beaten egg; coat with bread crumbs to cover completely. Place on the air fryer basket.
5. Bake for 30 minutes or until sausage is thoroughly cooked and no longer pink near egg.

Turkey Hoisin Burgers

Prep time: 10 minutes | Cook time: 20 minutes | Serves 4

454 g lean turkey mince
30 g whole-wheat bread crumbs
60 ml hoisin sauce

2 tbsps. soy sauce
4 whole-wheat buns
Olive oil spray

1. In a large bowl, mix together the turkey, bread crumbs, hoisin sauce, and soy sauce.
2. Form the mixture into 4 equal patties. Cover with plastic wrap and refrigerate the patties for 30 minutes.
3. Preheat the air fryer to 190ºC. Spray the air fryer basket lightly with olive oil spray.
4. Place the patties in the air fryer basket in a single layer. Spray the patties lightly with olive oil spray.
5. Air fry for 10 minutes. Flip the patties over, lightly spray with olive oil spray, and air fry for an additional 5 to 10 minutes, until golden brown.
6. Place the patties on buns and top with your choice of low-calorie burger toppings like sliced tomatoes, onions, and cabbage slaw. Serve immediately.

Full English Breakfast

Prep time: 10 minutes | Cook time: 23 minutes | Serves 1

2 sausages
2-3 rashers of bacon
1 flat mushrooms
1-2 ripe tomatoes

1 thick slice of black pudding
1 large egg
1 slice of bread

1. Preheat the air fryer to 180ºC for 5 minutes.
2. Air fry sausages in the air fryer basket for 12 minutes, turning every 2-3 minutes.
3. Remove sausages from the air fryer and replace with mushroom, pudding and halved tomatoes.
4. Keep sausages warm on a hot plate.
5. Air fry mushroom, pudding and tomato in the air fryer basket for about 6 minutes, turning at halfway point.
6. Air fry bacon for 3 minutes until crispy.
7. Add eggs to the air fryer and fry to liking.
8. Bake the bread in air fryer to your desired brownness.
9. Assemble cooked foods on a plate.

Easy Sausage Pizza

Prep time: 10 minutes | Cook time: 6 minutes | Serves 4

2 tbsps. ketchup
1 pita bread
45 g sausage

227 g Mozzarella cheese
1 tsp. garlic powder
1 tbsp. olive oil

1. Preheat the air fryer to 170ºC.
2. Spread the ketchup over the pita bread.
3. Top with the sausage and cheese. Sprinkle with the garlic powder and olive oil.
4. Put the pizza in the air fryer basket and bake for 6 minutes.
5. Serve warm.

Pita and Pepperoni Pizza

Prep time: 10 minutes | Cook time: 6 minutes | Serves 1

1 tsp. olive oil
1 tbsp. pizza sauce
1 pita bread
6 pepperoni slices

55 g grated Mozzarella cheese
¼ tsp. garlic powder
¼ tsp. dried oregano

1. Preheat the air fryer to 180ºC. Grease the air fryer basket with olive oil.
2. Spread the pizza sauce on top of the pita bread. Put the pepperoni slices over the sauce, followed by the Mozzarella cheese.
3. Season with garlic powder and oregano.
4. Put the pita pizza inside the air fryer and place a trivet on top.
5. Bake in the preheated air fryer for 6 minutes and serve.

Scone, Jam and Clotted Cream

Prep time: 10 minutes | Cook time: 15-20 minutes | Serves 5

250 g self-raising flour
120 ml 7-up / sprite
120 ml whipping cream

50 g caster sugar
To serve: Jam and clotted cream
To glaze: Milk or egg wash

1. Sieve flour in a mixing bowl.
2. Add lemonade, sugar and cream.
3. Mix together to combine ingredients. Be careful not to overmix.
4. Dredge some flour on a flat surface and knead the dough.
5. Use a scone cutter to cut individual scones.
6. Place scones in the air fryer basket with a 2 cm space between them.
7. Glaze scones with milk or egg wash and cook at 180ºC for 15-20 minutes.
8. Once the tops are golden, place scones on a wire cooling rack to cool.
9. Once cooled, serve with jam and clotted cream.

Oat and Chia Porridge

Prep time: 10 minutes | Cook time: 5 minutes | Serves 4

2 tbsps. peanut butter
4 tbsps. honey
1 tbsp. butter, melted

960 ml milk
312 g oats
160 g chia seeds

1. Preheat the air fryer to 200ºC.
2. Put the peanut butter, honey, butter, and milk in a bowl and stir to mix. Add the oats and chia seeds and stir.
3. Transfer the mixture to a bowl and bake in the air fryer for 5 minutes. Give another stir before serving.

Pig in Blankets

Prep time: <5 minutes | Cook time: 15-20 minutes | Serves 4-6

12 rashers
12 pork sausages
1 tbsp. clear honey

½ tbsp. grainy mustard
1 tbsp. chopped rosemary

1. Preheat the air fryer to 180ºC and cover the air fryer basket with foil.
2. Wrap a rasher of around each sausage and put on the basket. Place the honey, grainy mustard and chopped rosemary in a small pan and gently heat until the bubbling.
3. Brush the mixture over the sausages and air fry for 15-18 minutes until lightly browned. Serve, garnished with a little more chopped rosemary.

Tomato and Mozzarella Bruschetta

Prep time: 5 minutes | Cook time: 4 minutes | Serves 1

6 small loaf slices
100 g tomatoes, finely chopped
85 g Mozzarella cheese, grated

1 tbsp. fresh basil, chopped
1 tbsp. olive oil

1. Preheat the air fryer to 180ºC.
2. Put the loaf slices inside the air fryer and air fry for about 3 minutes.
3. Add the tomato, Mozzarella, basil, and olive oil on top.
4. Air fry for an additional minute before serving.

14 Chapter 3 Sandwiches and Casseroles

Chapter 3 Sandwiches and Casseroles

Cheesy Greens Sandwich

Prep time: 15 minutes | Cook time: 10 to 13 minutes | Serves 4

35 g chopped mixed greens
2 garlic cloves, thinly sliced
2 tsps. olive oil
2 slices low-sodium low-fat Swiss cheese
4 slices low-sodium whole-wheat bread
Cooking spray

1. Preheat the air fryer to 200ºC.
2. In the air fryer basket, mix the greens, garlic, and olive oil. Air fry for 4 to 5 minutes, stirring once, until the vegetables are tender. Drain, if necessary.
3. Make 2 sandwiches, dividing half of the greens and 1 slice of Swiss cheese between 2 slices of bread. Lightly spray the outsides of the sandwiches with cooking spray.
4. Bake the sandwiches in the air fryer for 6 to 8 minutes, turning with tongs halfway through, until the bread is toasted and the cheese melts.
5. Cut each sandwich in half and serve.

Veggie Pita Sandwich

Prep time: 10 minutes | Cook time: 9 to 12 minutes | Serves 4

1 baby aubergine, peeled and chopped
1 red pepper, sliced
30 g diced red onion
35 g shredded carrot
1 tsp. olive oil
90 glow-fat Greek yogurt
½ tsp. dried tarragon
2 low-sodium whole-wheat pita breads, halved crosswise

1. Preheat the air fryer to 200ºC.
2. In a baking dish, stir together the aubergine, red pepper, red onion, carrot, and olive oil. Put the vegetable mixture into the air fryer basket and roast for 7 to 9 minutes, stirring once, until the vegetables are tender. Drain if necessary.
3. In a small bowl, thoroughly mix the yogurt and tarragon until well combined.
4. Stir the yogurt mixture into the vegetables. Stuff one-fourth of this mixture into each pita pocket.
5. Place the sandwiches in the air fryer and bake for 2 to 3 minutes, or until the bread is toasted.
6. Serve immediately.

Prawn Green Casserole

Prep time: 15 minutes | Cook time: 22 minutes | Serves 4

454 g prawns, cleaned and deveined
210 g cauliflower, cut into florets
2 green pepper, sliced
1 shallot, sliced
2 tbsps. sesame oil
225 g tomato paste
Cooking spray

1. Preheat the air fryer to 180ºC. Spritz a baking dish with cooking spray.
2. Arrange the prawns and vegetables in the baking dish. Then, drizzle the sesame oil over the vegetables. Pour the tomato paste over the vegetables.
3. Bake for 10 minutes in the preheated air fryer. Stir with a large spoon and bake for a further 12 minutes.
4. Serve warm.

Cheesy Chicken Sandwich

Prep time: 10 minutes | Cook time: 5 to 7 minutes | Serves 1

50 g chicken, cooked and shredded
2 Mozzarella slices
1 hamburger bun
15 g shredded cabbage
1 tsp. mayonnaise
2 tsps. butter, melted
1 tsp. olive oil
½ tsp. balsamic vinegar
¼ tsp. smoked paprika
¼ tsp. black pepper
¼ tsp. garlic powder
Pinch of salt

1. Preheat the air fryer to 190ºC.
2. Brush some butter onto the outside of the hamburger bun.
3. In a bowl, coat the chicken with the garlic powder, salt, pepper, and paprika.
4. In a separate bowl, stir together the mayonnaise, olive oil, cabbage, and balsamic vinegar to make coleslaw.
5. Slice the bun in two. Start building the sandwich, starting with the chicken, followed by the Mozzarella, the coleslaw, and finally the top bun.
6. Transfer the sandwich to the air fryer and bake for 5 to 7 minutes.
7. Serve immediately.

Spinach Casserole

Prep time: 10 minutes | Cook time: 20 minutes | Serves 4

1 (383-g) can spinach, drained and squeezed
225 g cottage cheese
2 large eggs, beaten
55 g crumbled feta cheese
2 tbsps. plain flour

2 tbsps. butter, melted
1 clove garlic, minced, or more to taste
1 ½ tsps. onion powder
⅛ tsp. ground nutmeg
Cooking spray

1. Preheat the air fryer to 190ºC. Grease an 16-cm pie pan with cooking spray and set aside.
2. Combine spinach, cottage cheese, eggs, feta cheese, flour, butter, garlic, onion powder, and nutmeg in a bowl. Stir until all ingredients are well incorporated. Pour into the prepared pie pan.
3. Air fry until the centre is set, 18 to 20 minutes.
4. Serve warm.

Western Prosciutto Casserole

Prep time: 5 minutes | Cook time: 10 minutes | Serves 2

70 g day-old whole grain bread, cubed
3 large eggs, beaten
2 tbsps. water
⅛ tsp. salt

28 g prosciutto, roughly chopped
28 g Pepper Jack cheese, roughly chopped
1 tbsp. chopped fresh chives
Nonstick cooking spray

1. Preheat the air fryer to 180ºC.
2. Spray a baking dish with nonstick cooking spray, then place the bread cubes in the dish. Transfer the baking dish to the air fryer.
3. In a medium bowl, stir together the beaten eggs and water, then stir in the salt, prosciutto, cheese, and chives.
4. Pour the egg mixture over the bread cubes and bake for 10 minutes, or until the eggs are set and the top is golden brown.
5. Serve warm.

Bacon and Pepper Sandwich

Prep time: 10 minutes | Cook time: 6 minutes | Serves 4

75 g spicy barbecue sauce
2 tbsps. honey
8 slices cooked bacon, cut into thirds
1 red pepper, sliced

1 yellow pepper, sliced
3 pita pockets, cut in half
40 g torn butter lettuce leaves
2 tomatoes, sliced

1. Preheat the air fryer to 180ºC.
2. In a small bowl, combine the barbecue sauce and the honey. Brush this mixture lightly onto the bacon slices and the red and yellow pepper slices.
3. Put the peppers into the air fryer basket and roast for 4 minutes. Then shake the basket, add the bacon, and roast for 2 minutes or until the bacon is browned and the peppers are tender.
4. Fill the pita halves with the bacon, peppers, any remaining barbecue sauce, lettuce, and tomatoes, and serve immediately.

Creamy Tomato Casserole

Prep time: 5 minutes | Cook time: 30 minutes | Serves 4

5 eggs
2 tbsps. heavy cream
3 tbsps. chunky tomato sauce

2 tbsps. grated Parmesan cheese, plus more for topping

1. Preheat the air fryer to 180ºC.
2. Combine the eggs and cream in a bowl.
3. Mix in the tomato sauce and add the cheese.
4. Spread into a glass baking dish and bake in the preheated air fryer for 30 minutes.
5. Top with extra cheese and serve.

Baked Cheese Sandwich

Prep time: 5 minutes | Cook time: 8 minutes | Serves 2

2 tbsps. mayonnaise
4 thick slices sourdough bread

4 thick slices Brie cheese
8 slices hot capicola

1. Preheat the air fryer to 180ºC.
2. Spread the mayonnaise on one side of each slice of bread. Place 2 slices of bread in the air fryer basket, mayonnaise-side down.
3. Place the slices of Brie and capicola on the bread and cover with the remaining two slices of bread, mayonnaise-side up.
4. Bake for 8 minutes, or until the cheese has melted.
5. Serve immediately.

Chicken and Mushroom Casserole

Prep time: 15 minutes | Cook time: 20 minutes | Serves 4

4 chicken breasts
1 tbsp. curry powder
240 ml coconut milk
Salt, to taste

1 broccoli, cut into florets
90 g mushrooms
45 g shredded Parmesan cheese
Cooking spray

1. Preheat the air fryer to 180ºC. Spritz a casserole dish with cooking spray.
2. Cube the chicken breasts and combine with curry powder and coconut milk in a bowl. Season with salt.
3. Add the broccoli and mushroom and mix well.
4. Pour the mixture into the casserole dish. Top with the cheese.
5. Transfer to the air fryer and bake for about 20 minutes.
6. Serve warm.

Smoky Chicken Sandwich

Prep time: 10 minutes | Cook time: 11 minutes | Serves 2

2 boneless, skinless chicken breasts (227 g each), sliced horizontally in half and separated into 4 thinner cutlets
Salt and freshly ground black pepper, to taste
60 g plain flour
3 large eggs, lightly beaten
60 g dried bread crumbs
1 tbsp. smoked paprika
Cooking spray
110 g marinara sauce
170 g smoked Mozzarella cheese, grated
2 store-bought soft, sesame-seed hamburger or Italian buns, split

1. Preheat the air fryer to 180ºC.
2. Season the chicken cutlets all over with salt and pepper. Set up three shallow bowls: Place the flour in the first bowl, the eggs in the second, and stir together the bread crumbs and smoked paprika in the third. Coat the chicken pieces in the flour, then dip fully in the egg. Dredge in the paprika bread crumbs, then transfer to a wire rack set over a baking sheet and spray both sides liberally with cooking spray.
3. Transfer 2 of the chicken cutlets to the air fryer and air fry for 6 minutes, or until beginning to brown. Spread each cutlet with 2 tbsps. of the marinara sauce and sprinkle with one-quarter of the smoked Mozzarella. Increase the temperature to 204ºC and air fry for 5 minutes more, or until the chicken is cooked through and crisp and the cheese is melted and golden brown.
4. Transfer the cutlets to a plate, stack on top of each other, and place inside a bun. Repeat with the remaining chicken cutlets, marinara, smoked Mozzarella, and bun.
5. Serve the sandwiches warm.

Chapter 4 Vegetables

Basmati Risotto

Prep time: 10 minutes | Cook time: 30 minutes | Serves 2

1 onion, diced
1 small carrot, diced
480 ml vegetable stock, boiling
40 g grated Cheddar cheese
1 clove garlic, minced
135 g long-grain basmati rice
1 tbsp. olive oil
1 tbsp. unsalted butter

1. Preheat the air fryer to 200ºC.
2. Grease a baking tin with oil and stir in the butter, garlic, carrot, and onion.
3. Put the tin in the air fryer and bake for 4 minutes.
4. Pour in the rice and bake for a further 4 minutes, stirring three times throughout the baking time.
5. Turn the temperature down to 160ºC.
6. Add the vegetable stock and give the dish a gentle stir. Bake for 22 minutes, leaving the air fryer uncovered.
7. Pour in the cheese, stir once more and serve.

Simple Sweet Potato Soufflé

Prep time: 10 minutes | Cook time: 30 minutes | Serves 4

1 sweet potato, baked and mashed
2 tbsps. unsalted butter, divided
1 large egg, separated
60 ml whole milk
½ tsp. salt

1. Preheat the air fryer to 165ºC.
2. In a medium bowl, combine the sweet potato, 1 tbsp. of melted butter, egg yolk, milk, and salt. Set aside.
3. In a separate medium bowl, whisk the egg white until stiff peaks form.
4. Using a spatula, gently fold the egg white into the sweet potato mixture.
5. Coat the inside of four 6-cm ramekins with the remaining 1 tbsp. of butter, then fill each ramekin halfway full. Place 2 ramekins in the air fryer basket and bake for 15 minutes. Repeat this process with the remaining ramekins.
6. Remove the ramekins from the air fryer and allow to cool on a wire rack for 10 minutes before serving.

Black Bean and Tomato Chili

Prep time: 15 minutes | Cook time: 23 minutes | Serves 6

1 tbsp. olive oil
1 medium onion, diced
3 garlic cloves, minced
240 ml vegetable stock
3 cans black beans, drained and rinsed
2 cans diced tomatoes
2 chipotle peppers, chopped
2 tsps. cumin
2 tsps. chili powder
1 tsp. dried oregano
½ tsp. salt

1. Over a medium heat, fry the garlic and onions in the olive oil for 3 minutes.
2. Add the remaining ingredients, stirring constantly and scraping the bottom to prevent sticking.
3. Preheat the air fryer to 200ºC.
4. Take a dish and place the mixture inside. Put a sheet of aluminum foil on top.
5. Transfer to the air fryer and bake for 20 minutes.
6. When ready, plate up and serve immediately.

Beetroot Salad with Lemon Vinaigrette

Prep time: 10 minutes | Cook time: 12 to 15 minutes | Serves 4

6 medium red and golden beetroots, peeled and sliced
1 tsp. olive oil
¼ tsp. salt
110 g crumbled Feta cheese
160 g mixed greens
Cooking spray
Vinaigrette:
2 tsps. olive oil
2 tbsps. chopped fresh chives
Juice of 1 lemon

1. Preheat the air fryer to 180ºC.
2. In a large bowl, toss the beetroot, olive oil, and salt.
3. Spray the air fryer basket with cooking spray, then place the beetroot in the basket and air fry for 12 to 15 minutes or until tender.
4. While the beetroot cooks, make the vinaigrette in a large bowl by whisking together the olive oil, lemon juice, and chives.
5. Remove the beetroot from the air fryer, toss in the vinaigrette, and allow to cool for 5 minutes. Add the Feta and serve on top of the mixed greens.

Herbed Radishes

Prep time: 5 minutes | Cook time: 10 minutes | Serves 2

454 g radishes	¼ tsp. dried oregano
2 tbsps. unsalted butter, melted	½ tsp. dried parsley
	½ tsp. garlic powder

1. Preheat the air fryer to 180ºC. Prepare the radishes by cutting off their tops and bottoms and quartering them.
2. In a bowl, combine the butter, dried oregano, dried parsley, and garlic powder. Toss with the radishes to coat.
3. Transfer the radishes to the air fryer and air fry for 10 minutes, shaking the basket at the halfway point to ensure the radishes air fry evenly through. The radishes are ready when they turn brown.
4. Serve immediately.

Air Fried Brussels Sprouts

Prep time: 5 minutes | Cook time: 10 minutes | Serves 1

454 g Brussels sprouts	1 tbsp. unsalted butter, melted
1 tbsp. coconut oil, melted	

1. Preheat the air fryer to 200ºC.
2. Prepare the Brussels sprouts by halving them, discarding any loose leaves.
3. Combine with the melted coconut oil and transfer to the air fryer.
4. Air fry for 10 minutes, giving the basket a good shake throughout the air frying time to brown them up if desired.
5. The sprouts are ready when they are partially caramelized. Remove them from the air fryer and serve with a topping of melted butter before serving.

Cauliflower Faux Rice

Prep time: 15 minutes | Cook time: 40 minutes | Serves 8

1 large head cauliflower, rinsed and drained, cut into florets	130 g peas
½ lemon, juiced	1 egg, beaten
2 garlic cloves, minced	4 tbsps. soy sauce
2 (227-g) cans mushrooms	1 tbsp. peanut oil
1 (227-g) can water chestnuts	1 tbsp. sesame oil
	1 tbsp. minced fresh ginger
	Cooking spray

1. Preheat the air fryer to 180ºC.
2. Mix the peanut oil, soy sauce, sesame oil, minced ginger, lemon juice, and minced garlic to combine well.
3. In a food processor, pulse the florets in small batches to break them down to resemble rice grains. Pour into the air fryer basket.
4. Drain the chestnuts and roughly chop them. Pour into the basket. Air fry for 20 minutes.
5. In the meantime, drain the mushrooms. Add the mushrooms and the peas to the air fryer and continue to air fry for another 15 minutes.
6. Lightly spritz a frying pan with cooking spray. Prepare an omelet with the beaten egg, ensuring it is firm. Lay on a cutting board and slice it up.
7. When the cauliflower is ready, throw in the omelet and bake for an additional 5 minutes. Serve hot.

Beef Stuffed Pepper

Prep time: 20 minutes | Cook time: 15 minutes | Serves 4

2 garlic cloves, minced	60 g shredded cheese, divided
1 small onion, chopped	130 g cooked rice
Cooking spray	2 tsps. Worcestershire sauce
454 g beef mince	227 g tomato sauce
1 tsp. dried basil	4 peppers, tops removed
½ tsp. chili powder	
1 tsp. black pepper	
1 tsp. garlic salt	

1. Grease a frying pan with cooking spray and fry the onion and garlic over a medium heat.
2. Stir in the beef, basil, chili powder, black pepper, and garlic salt, combining everything well. Air fry until the beef is nicely browned, before taking the pan off the heat.
3. Add half of the cheese, the rice, Worcestershire sauce, and tomato sauce and stir to combine.
4. Spoon equal amounts of the beef mixture into the four peppers, filling them entirely.
5. Preheat the air fryer to 205ºC.
6. Spritz the air fryer basket with cooking spray.
7. Put the stuffed peppers in the basket and air fry for 11 minutes.
8. Add the remaining cheese on top of each pepper and air fry for a further 2 minutes. When the cheese is melted and the peppers are piping hot, serve immediately.

Green Beans with Shallot

Prep time: 10 minutes | Cook time: 10 minutes | Serves 4

680 g green beans, stems removed and blanched
1 tbsp. salt
227 g shallots, peeled
and cut into quarters
½ tsp. ground white pepper
2 tbsps. olive oil

1. Preheat the air fryer to 200ºC.
2. Coat the vegetables with the rest of the ingredients in a bowl.
3. Transfer to the air fryer basket and air fry for 10 minutes, making sure the green beans achieve a light brown colour.
4. Serve hot.

Courgette Balls

Prep time: 5 minutes | Cook time: 10 minutes | Serves 4

4 courgettes
1 egg
47 g grated Parmesan
cheese
1 tbsp. Italian herbs
80 g grated coconut

1. Thinly grate the courgettes and dry with a cheesecloth, ensuring to remove all the moisture.
2. In a bowl, combine the courgettes with the egg, Parmesan, Italian herbs, and grated coconut, mixing well to incorporate everything. Using the hands, mold the mixture into balls.
3. Preheat the air fryer to 200ºC.
4. Lay the courgette balls in the air fryer basket and air fry for 10 minutes.
5. Serve hot.

Mediterranean Air Fried Veggies

Prep time: 10 minutes | Cook time: 6 minutes | Serves 4

1 large courgette, sliced
200 g cherry tomatoes, halved
1 parsnip, sliced
1 green pepper, sliced
1 carrot, sliced
1 tsp. mixed herbs
1 tsp. mustard
1 tsp. garlic purée
6 tbsps. olive oil
Salt and ground black pepper, to taste

1. Preheat the air fryer to 200ºC.
2. Combine all the ingredients in a bowl, making sure to coat the vegetables well.
3. Transfer to the air fryer and air fry for 6 minutes, ensuring the vegetables are tender and browned.
4. Serve immediately.

Cauliflower, Chickpea, and Avocado Mash

Prep time: 10 minutes | Cook time: 25 minutes | Serves 4

1 medium head cauliflower, cut into florets
1 can chickpeas, drained and rinsed
1 tbsp. extra-virgin olive
oil
2 tbsps. lemon juice
Salt and ground black pepper, to taste
4 flatbreads, toasted
2 ripe avocados, mashed

1. Preheat the air fryer to 220ºC.
2. In a bowl, mix the chickpeas, cauliflower, lemon juice and olive oil. Sprinkle salt and pepper as desired.
3. Put inside the air fryer basket and air fry for 25 minutes.
4. Spread on top of the flatbread along with the mashed avocado. Sprinkle with more pepper and salt and serve.

Prosciutto Mini Mushroom Pizza

Prep time: 10 minutes | Cook time: 5 minutes | Serves 3

3 portobello mushroom caps, cleaned and scooped
3 tbsps. olive oil
Pinch of salt
Pinch of dried Italian
seasonings
3 tbsps. tomato sauce
3 tbsps. shredded Mozzarella cheese
12 slices prosciutto

1. Preheat the air fryer to 165ºC.
2. Season both sides of the portobello mushrooms with a drizzle of olive oil, then sprinkle salt and the Italian seasonings on the insides.
3. With a knife, spread the tomato sauce evenly over the mushroom, before adding the Mozzarella on top.
4. Put the portobello in the air fryer basket and place in the air fryer.
5. Air fry for 1 minute, before taking the air fryer basket out of the air fryer and putting the prosciutto slices on top.
6. Air fry for another 4 minutes.
7. Serve warm.

Easy Rosemary Green Beans

Prep time: 5 minutes | Cook time: 5 minutes | Serves 1

1 tbsp. butter, melted
2 tbsps. rosemary
½ tsp. salt

3 cloves garlic, minced
100 g chopped green beans

1. Preheat the air fryer to 200ºC.
2. Combine the melted butter with the rosemary, salt, and minced garlic. Toss in the green beans, coating them well.
3. Air fry for 5 minutes.
4. Serve immediately.

Bubble and Squeak

Prep time: 20 minutes | Cook time: 25 minutes | Serves 4

1 fresh egg, lightly beaten
1 tbsp. milk
2 tbsps. plain flour
150 g brussels sprouts, cooked and finely sliced

25 g butter
1 tbsp. olive oil
4 potatoes peeled, cooked and mashed
1 tsp. salt freshly ground

1. Cover the potatoes with cold water in a pan and bring to the boil, then simmer for 15-20 minutes or until completely tender when pierced with the tip of a sharp knife.
2. Strain the potatoes and add the butter and milk, mash well to ensure there are no lumps.
3. Add the sprouts to the mashed potato and add the flour and seasoning, pour in the beaten egg.
4. Using your hands combine all the ingredients together and turn out on to a lightly floured surface.
5. Use a rolling pin to flatten the mixture and take a scone cutter or ramekin to cut the mixture. Set aside.
6. Preheat the air fryer to 180ºC and spay the air fryer basket with oil.
7. Then place the patty shapes in the air fryer basket.
8. Air fry on each side for 4 minutes until golden down.

Kidney Beans Oatmeal in Peppers

Prep time: 15 minutes | Cook time: 6 minutes | Serves 2 to 4

2 large peppers, halved lengthwise, deseeded
2 tbsps. cooked kidney beans
2 tbsps. cooked chick peas
170 g cooked oatmeal
1 tsp. ground cumin

½ tsp. paprika
½ tsp. salt or to taste
¼ tsp. black pepper powder
65 g yogurt

1. Preheat the air fryer to 180ºC.
2. Put the peppers, cut-side down, in the air fryer basket. Air fry for 2 minutes.
3. Take the peppers out of the air fryer and let cool.
4. In a bowl, combine the rest of the ingredients.
5. Divide the mixture evenly and use each portion to stuff a pepper.
6. Return the stuffed peppers to the air fryer and continue to air fry for 4 minutes.
7. Serve hot.

Potatoes with Courgettes

Prep time: 10 minutes | Cook time: 45 minutes | Serves 4

2 potatoes, peeled and cubed
4 carrots, cut into chunks
1 head broccoli, cut into florets
4 courgettes, sliced thickly

Salt and ground black pepper, to taste
60 ml olive oil
1 tbsp. dry onion powder

1. Preheat the air fryer to 200ºC.
2. In a baking dish, add all the ingredients and combine well.
3. Bake for 45 minutes in the air fryer, ensuring the vegetables are soft and the sides have browned before serving.

Simple Buffalo Cauliflower

Prep time: 5 minutes | Cook time: 5 minutes | Serves 1

½ packet dry ranch seasoning
2 tbsps. salted butter, melted

100 g cauliflower florets
62 g buffalo sauce

1. Preheat the air fryer to 200ºC.
2. In a bowl, combine the dry ranch seasoning and butter. Toss with the cauliflower florets to coat and transfer them to the air fryer.
3. Roast for 5 minutes, shaking the basket occasionally to ensure the florets roast evenly.
4. Remove the cauliflower from the air fryer, pour the buffalo sauce over it, and serve.

Chapter 5 Fish and Seafood

Lemony Prawn and Courgette

Prep time: 15 minutes | Cook time: 7 to 8 minutes | Serves 4

567 g extra-large raw prawn, peeled and deveined
2 medium courgette (227 g each), halved lengthwise and cut into 1-cm thick slices
1½ tbsps. olive oil
½ tsp. garlic salt
1½ tsps. dried oregano
⅛ tsp. crushed red pepper flakes (optional)
Juice of ½ lemon
1 tbsp. chopped fresh mint
1 tbsp. chopped fresh dill

1. Preheat the air fryer to 180ºC.
2. In a large bowl, combine the prawns, courgette, oil, garlic salt, oregano, and pepper flakes (if using) and toss to coat.
3. Working in batches, arrange a single layer of the prawn and courgette in the air fryer basket. Air fry for 7 to 8 minutes, shaking the basket halfway, until the courgette is golden and the prawns are cooked through.
4. Transfer to a serving dish and tent with foil while you air fry the remaining prawns and courgette.
5. Top with the lemon juice, mint, and dill and serve.

Blackened Salmon

Prep time: 10 minutes | Cook time: 5 to 7 minutes | Serves 4

Salmon:
1 tbsp. sweet paprika
½ tsp. cayenne pepper
1 tsp. garlic powder
1 tsp. dried oregano
1 tsp. dried thyme
¾ tsp. salt
⅛ tsp. freshly ground black pepper
Cooking spray
4 (170 g each) wild salmon fillets
Cucumber-Avocado

Salsa:
2 tbsps. chopped red onion
1½ tbsps. fresh lemon juice
1 tsp. extra-virgin olive oil
¼ tsp. plus ⅛ tsp. salt
Freshly ground black pepper, to taste
4 Persian cucumbers, diced
170 g Hass avocado, diced

1. For the salmon: In a small bowl, combine the paprika, cayenne, garlic powder, oregano, thyme, salt, and black pepper. Spray both sides of the fish with oil and rub all over. Coat the fish all over with the spices.
2. For the cucumber-avocado salsa: In a medium bowl, combine the red onion, lemon juice, olive oil, salt, and pepper. Let stand for 5 minutes, then add the cucumbers and avocado.
3. Preheat the air fryer to 200ºC.
4. Working in batches, arrange the salmon fillets skin side down in the air fryer basket. Air fry for 5 to 7 minutes, or until the fish flakes easily with a fork, depending on the thickness of the fish.
5. Serve topped with the salsa.

Fish Sandwich with Tartar Sauce

Prep time: 10 minutes | Cook time: 17 minutes | Serves 2

Tartar Sauce:
120 g mayonnaise
2 tbsps. dried minced onion
1 dill pickle spear, finely chopped
2 tsps. pickle juice
¼ tsp. salt
⅛ tsp. ground black
pepper
Fish:
2 tbsps. plain flour
1 egg, lightly beaten
125 g panko
2 tsps. lemon pepper
2 tilapia fillets
Cooking spray
2 hoagie rolls

1. Preheat the air fryer to 200ºC.
2. In a small bowl, combine the mayonnaise, dried minced onion, pickle, pickle juice, salt, and pepper.
3. Whisk to combine and chill in the refrigerator while you make the fish.
4. Place a parchment liner in the air fryer basket.
5. Scoop the flour out onto a plate; set aside.
6. Put the beaten egg in a medium shallow bowl.
7. On another plate, mix to combine the panko and lemon pepper.
8. Dredge the tilapia fillets in the flour, then dip in the egg, and then press into the panko mixture.
9. Place the prepared fillets on the liner in the air fryer in a single layer.
10. Spray lightly with cooking spray and air fry for 8 minutes. Carefully flip the fillets, spray with more cooking spray, and air fry for an additional 9 minutes, until golden and crispy.
11. Place each cooked fillet in a hoagie roll, top with a little bit of tartar sauce, and serve.

Crispy Coconut Prawn

Prep time: 15 minutes | Cook time: 8 minutes | Serves 4

Sweet Chili Mayo:
3 tbsps. mayonnaise
3 tbsps. Thai sweet chili sauce
1 tbsp. Sriracha sauce
Prawn:
45 g sweetened shredded coconut
75 g panko bread crumbs

Salt, to taste
2 tbsps. plain or gluten-free flour
2 large eggs
24 extra-jumbo prawns (454 g), peeled and deveined
Cooking spray

1. In a medium bowl, combine the mayonnaise, Thai sweet chili sauce, and Sriracha and mix well.
2. In a medium bowl, combine the coconut, panko, and ¼ tsp. salt. Place the flour in a shallow bowl. Whisk the eggs in another shallow bowl.
3. Season the prawns with ⅛ tsp. salt. Dip the prawns in the flour, shaking off any excess, then into the egg. Coat in the coconut-panko mixture, gently pressing to adhere, then transfer to a large plate. Spray both sides of the prawns with oil.
4. Preheat the air fryer to 180ºC.
5. Working in batches, arrange a single layer of the prawn in the air fryer basket. Air fry for about 8 minutes, flipping halfway, until the crust is golden brown and the prawn are cooked through.
6. Serve with the sweet chili mayo for dipping.

Classic Prawn Empanadas

Prep time: 10 minutes | Cook time: 8 minutes | Serves 5

227g raw prawn, peeled, deveined and chopped
20 g chopped red onion
1 spring onion, chopped
2 garlic cloves, minced
2 tbsps. minced red pepper
2 tbsps. chopped fresh coriander
½ tbsp. fresh lime juice

¼ tsp. sweet paprika
⅛ tsp. salt
⅛ tsp. crushed red pepper flakes (optional)
1 large egg, beaten
10 frozen Goya Empanada Discos, thawed
Cooking spray

1. In a medium bowl, combine the prawns, red onion, spring onion, garlic, pepper, coriander, lime juice, paprika, salt, and pepper flakes (if using).
2. In a small bowl, beat the egg with 1 tsp. water until smooth.
3. Place an empanada disc on a work surface and put 2 tbsps. of the prawn mixture in the centre. Brush the outer edges of the disc with the egg wash. Fold the disc over and gently press the edges to seal. Use a fork and press around the edges to crimp and seal completely. Brush the tops of the empanadas with the egg wash.
4. Preheat the air fryer to 190ºC.
5. Spray the bottom of the air fryer basket with cooking spray to prevent sticking. Working in batches, arrange a single layer of the empanadas in the air fryer basket and air fry for about 8 minutes, flipping halfway, until golden brown and crispy.
6. Serve hot.

Remoulade Crab Cakes

Prep time: 15 minutes | Cook time: 10 minutes | Serves 4

Remoulade:
182 g mayonnaise
2 tsps. Dijon mustard
1½ tsps. yellow mustard
1 tsp. vinegar
¼ tsp. hot sauce
1 tsp. tiny capers, drained and chopped
¼ tsp. salt
⅛ tsp. ground black pepper
Crab Cakes:
125 g bread crumbs,

divided
2 tbsps. mayonnaise
1 spring onion, finely chopped
170 g crab meat
2 tbsps. pasteurized egg product (liquid eggs in a carton)
2 tsps. lemon juice
½ tsp. red pepper flakes
½ tsp. Old Bay seasoning
Cooking spray

1. Preheat the air fryer to 200ºC.
2. In a small bowl, whisk to combine the mayonnaise, Dijon mustard, yellow mustard, vinegar, hot sauce, capers, salt, and pepper.
3. Refrigerate for at least 1 hour before serving.
4. Place a parchment liner in the air fryer basket.
5. In a large bowl, mix to combine 65 g of bread crumbs with the Remoulade and spring onion. Set the other 60 g of bread crumbs aside in a small bowl.
6. Add the crab meat, egg product, lemon juice, red pepper flakes, and Old Bay seasoning to the large bowl, and stir to combine.
7. Divide the crab mixture into 4 portions, and form into patties.
8. Dredge each patty in the remaining bread crumbs to coat.
9. Place the prepared patties on the liner in the air fryer in a single layer.
10. Spray lightly with cooking spray and air fry for 5 minutes. Flip the crab cakes over, air fry for another 5 minutes, until golden, and serve.

Garlic Scallops

Prep time: 10 minutes | Cook time: 10 to 15 minutes | Serves 4

2 tsps. olive oil
1 packet dry zesty Italian dressing mix
1 tsp. minced garlic
454 g small scallops, patted dry
Cooking spray

1. Preheat the air fryer to 200ºC.
2. Spray the air fryer basket lightly with cooking spray.
3. In a large zip-top plastic bag, combine the olive oil, Italian dressing mix, and garlic.
4. Add the scallops, seal the zip-top bag, and coat the scallops in the seasoning mixture.
5. Place the scallops in the air fryer basket and lightly spray with cooking spray.
6. Air fry for 5 minutes, shake the basket, and air fry for 5 to 10 more minutes, or until the scallops reach an internal temperature of 50ºC.
7. Serve immediately.

Crab Cake Sandwich

Prep time: 15 minutes | Cook time: 10 minutes | Serves 4

Crab Cakes:
62 g panko bread crumbs
1 large egg, beaten
1 large egg white
1 tbsp. mayonnaise
1 tsp. Dijon mustard
15 g minced fresh parsley
1 tbsp. fresh lemon juice
½ tsp. Old Bay seasoning
⅛ tsp. sweet paprika
⅛ tsp. salt
Freshly ground black

pepper, to taste
283 g lump crab meat
Cooking spray
Cajun Mayo:
60 g mayonnaise
1 tbsp. minced dill pickle
1 tsp. fresh lemon juice
¾ tsp. Cajun seasoning
For Serving:
4 Boston lettuce leaves
4 whole wheat potato buns or gluten-free buns

1. For the crab cakes: In a large bowl, combine the panko, whole egg, egg white, mayonnaise, mustard, parsley, lemon juice, Old Bay, paprika, salt, and pepper to taste and mix well. Fold in the crab meat, being careful not to over mix. Gently shape into 4 round patties, about ½ cup each, 1 ½ cm thick. Spray both sides with oil.
2. Preheat the air fryer to 190ºC.
3. Working in batches, place the crab cakes in the air fryer basket. Air fry for about 10 minutes, flipping halfway, until the edges are golden.
4. Meanwhile, for the Cajun mayo: In a small bowl, combine the mayonnaise, pickle, lemon juice, and Cajun seasoning.
5. To serve: Place a lettuce leaf on each bun bottom and top with a crab cake and a generous tbsp. of Cajun mayonnaise. Add the bun top and serve.

Fish and Chips

Prep time: 15 minutes | Cook time: 30 minutes | Serves 4

cooking spray
4 fillets of cod (200 g per person)
For the Batter:
250 g plain flour
50 g corn flour
1 L bottle of sparkling water
1 tsp. sea salt
For the Chips:
6 large potatoes

1. Preheat the air fryer to 150ºC and spay the air fryer basket with oil.
2. Prepare the batter about twenty minute or so before you are ready to cook and leave in the fridge to settle.
3. Put the 225 g flour into a large bowl, add the corn flour and the salt and mix gently.
4. Add the sparkling water little by little while stirring gently with a whisk. When the batter will coat the back of a spoon it's ready. If it's too watery add a little flour if it's too stodgy add a little water. It will bubble up as you whisk don't worry this is what makes the batter light and airy. It's all in the bubbles.
5. You don't need to whisk it perfectly as some lumps of flour will add to the crunch once cooked. Put it in the fridge for 20 minutes or so.
6. Skin the potatoes and cut into thin slices. Rinse in cold water and dry thoroughly in a tea towel. Place the chips in the air fryer basket.
7. Air fry the chips for 5 minutes or until soft in the middle. Leave to one side to cool.
8. Cut the fish fillets into smaller pieces of roughly equal size.
9. Increase the air fryer to 190°C.
10. Add the a pinch of sea salt to the remaining flour. Take your pieces of fish and dip in the flour. Shake off the excess flour and dip in the batter.
11. Air fry the fish for 5 minutes, shaking the basket halfway.
12. Take one of the pieces out and break to check if it's cooked.
13. Finish off your chips in the air fryer for about 2 minutes they are already cooked so they just need to brown up and get crispy.
14. Place the fish and the chips onto some kitchen paper to take off any excess oil.

Roasted Cod with Sesame Seeds

Prep time: 5 minutes | Cook time: 7 to 9 minutes | Makes 1 fillet

1 tbsp. reduced-sodium soy sauce	Cooking spray
2 tsps. honey	170 g fresh cod fillet
	1 tsp. sesame seeds

1. Preheat the air fryer to 180ºC.
2. In a small bowl, combine the soy sauce and honey.
3. Spray the air fryer basket with cooking spray, then place the cod in the basket, brush with the soy mixture, and sprinkle sesame seeds on top. Roast for 7 to 9 minutes or until opaque.
4. Remove the fish and allow to cool on a wire rack for 5 minutes before serving.

Cullen Skink

Prep time: 30 minutes | Cook time: 30 minutes | Serves 2

cooking spray	(approximately 2 fillets)
25 g butter	300 ml whole milk
1 medium onion	300 ml boiling water
400 g potatoes	Optional – Parsley to
280 g smoked haddock	garnish

1. Preheat the air fryer to 180ºC and spay an ovenproof dish with oil.
2. Put the milk and smoked haddock skin-up (if there is any) into one pan and allow to sit. The milk should cover the whole fish. Don't turn the heat on yet.
3. Finely chop an onion and peel and cube the potatoes.
4. Add the butter and onion to the dish and air fry for around 3 minutes until the onion is soft but not brown.
5. Add the potatoes and cook for a minute before pouring in 300 ml of boiling water. Cover and allow to simmer for 15 minutes or so until the potatoes are cooked through.
6. Meanwhile, heat the milk and haddock gradually, moving the milk around with a wooden spoon every now and then so it doesn't stick. It should take about 5 minutes or so for the milk to heat up and then cook the fish for a further 5 minutes.
7. Remove the smoked haddock from the milk with a slotted spoon and keep the milk to one side.
8. Allow the fish to cool slightly and any skin or bones and discard them.
9. Take a masher or fork and roughly mash about a quarter of the potatoes. You can just do this in the dish, no need to take any out.
10. Add the milk to the dish of potatoes and onions and stir for a few minutes to combine.
11. Use a fork to separate the smoked haddock into large chunks then add to the dish and stir gently through. Salt and pepper to taste.
12. Add parsley or cream if you choose to.

Fish Croquettes with Lemon-Dill Aioli

Prep time: 15 minutes | Cook time: 10 minutes | Serves 4

Croquettes:	94 g plus 2 tbsps. bread
3 large eggs, divided	crumbs, divided
340 g raw cod fillet, flaked apart with two forks	1 tsp. fresh lemon juice
	1 tsp. salt
60 ml low-fat milk	½ tsp. dried thyme
96 g boxed instant mashed potatoes	¼ tsp. freshly ground black pepper
2 tsps. olive oil	Cooking spray
24 g chopped fresh dill	**Lemon-Dill Aioli:**
1 shallot, minced	5 tbsps. mayonnaise
1 large garlic clove, minced	Juice of ½ lemon
	1 tbsp. chopped fresh dill

1. For the croquettes: In a medium bowl, lightly beat 2 of the eggs. Add the fish, milk, instant mashed potatoes, olive oil, dill, shallot, garlic, 2 tbsps. of the bread crumbs, lemon juice, salt, thyme, and pepper. Mix to thoroughly combine. Place in the refrigerator for 30 minutes.
2. For the lemon-dill aioli: In a small bowl, combine the mayonnaise, lemon juice, and dill. Set aside.
3. Measure out about 3½ tbsps. of the fish mixture and gently roll in your hands to form a log about 6-cm long. Repeat to make a total of 12 logs.
4. Beat the remaining egg in a small bowl. Place the remaining 94 g bread crumbs in a separate bowl. Dip the croquettes in the egg, then coat in the bread crumbs, gently pressing to adhere. Place on a work surface and spray both sides with cooking spray.
5. Preheat the air fryer to 180ºC.
6. Working in batches, arrange a single layer of the croquettes in the air fryer basket. Air fry for about 10 minutes, flipping halfway, until golden.
7. Serve with the aioli for dipping.

Roasted Fish with Almond-Lemon Crumbs

Prep time: 10 minutes | Cook time: 7 to 8 minutes | Serves 4

68 g raw whole almonds
1 spring onion, finely chopped
Grated zest and juice of 1 lemon
½ tbsp. extra-virgin olive oil

¾ tsp. salt, divided
Freshly ground black pepper, to taste
4 (170 g each) skinless fish fillets
Cooking spray
1 tsp. Dijon mustard

1. In a food processor, pulse the almonds to coarsely chop. Transfer to a small bowl and add the spring onion, lemon zest, and olive oil. Season with ¼ tsp. of the salt and pepper to taste and mix to combine.
2. Spray the top of the fish with oil and squeeze the lemon juice over the fish. Season with the remaining ½ tsp. salt and pepper to taste. Spread the mustard on top of the fish. Dividing evenly, press the almond mixture onto the top of the fillets to adhere.
3. Preheat the air fryer to 190ºC.
4. Working in batches, place the fillets in the air fryer basket in a single layer. Air fry for 7 to 8 minutes, until the crumbs start to brown and the fish is cooked through. Serve immediately.

Tortilla Prawn Tacos

Prep time: 10 minutes | Cook time: 6 minutes | Serves 4

Spicy Mayo:
3 tbsps. mayonnaise
1 tbsp. Louisiana-style hot pepper sauce
Coriander-Lime Slaw:
50 g shredded green cabbage
½ small red onion, thinly sliced
1 small jalapeño, thinly sliced
2 tbsps. chopped fresh

coriander
Juice of 1 lime
¼ tsp. salt
Prawn:
1 large egg, beaten
30 g crushed tortilla chips
24 jumbo prawn (454 g), peeled and deveined
⅛ tsp. salt
Cooking spray
8 corn tortillas, for serving

1. For the spicy mayo: In a small bowl, mix the mayonnaise and hot pepper sauce.
2. For the coriander-lime slaw: In a large bowl, toss together the cabbage, onion, jalapeño, coriander, lime juice, and salt to combine. Cover and refrigerate to chill.
3. For the prawn: Place the egg in a shallow bowl and

the crushed tortilla chips in another. Season the prawn with the salt. Dip the prawn in the egg, then in the crumbs, pressing gently to adhere. Place on a work surface and spray both sides with oil.
4. Preheat the air fryer to 180ºC.
5. Working in batches, arrange a single layer of the prawn in the air fryer basket. Air fry for 6 minutes, flipping halfway, until golden and cooked through in the centre.
6. To serve, place 2 tortillas on each plate and top each with 3 prawn. Top each taco with ¼ cup slaw, then drizzle with spicy mayo.

Salmon Burgers

Prep time: 15 minutes | Cook time: 12 minutes | Serves 5

Lemon-Caper Rémoulade:
120 g mayonnaise
2 tbsps. minced drained capers
2 tbsps. chopped fresh parsley
2 tsps. fresh lemon juice
Salmon Patties:
454 g wild salmon fillet, skinned and pin bones removed
6 tbsps. panko bread crumbs
20 g minced red onion

plus 20 g slivered for serving
1 garlic clove, minced
1 large egg, lightly beaten
1 tbsp. Dijon mustard
1 tsp. fresh lemon juice
1 tbsp. chopped fresh parsley
½ tsp. salt
For Serving:
5 whole wheat potato buns or gluten-free buns
10 butter lettuce leaves

1. For the lemon-caper rémoulade: In a small bowl, combine the mayonnaise, capers, parsley, and lemon juice and mix well.
2. For the salmon patties: Cut off a 113-g piece of the salmon and transfer to a food processor. Pulse until it becomes pasty. With a sharp knife, chop the remaining salmon into small cubes.
3. In a medium bowl, combine the chopped and processed salmon with the panko, minced red onion, garlic, egg, mustard, lemon juice, parsley, and salt. Toss gently to combine. Form the mixture into 5 patties about 1 ½ cm thick. Refrigerate for at least 30 minutes.
4. Preheat the air fryer to 200ºC.
5. Working in batches, place the patties in the air fryer basket. Air fry for about 12 minutes, gently flipping halfway, until golden and cooked through.
6. To serve, transfer each patty to a bun. Top each with 2 lettuce leaves, 2 tbsps. of the rémoulade, and the slivered red onions.

Chapter 6 Meats

Carne Asada Tacos

Prep time: 5 minutes | Cook time: 14 minutes | Serves 4

80 ml olive oil
680 g flank steak
Salt and freshly ground black pepper, to taste
80 ml freshly squeezed lime juice
20 g chopped fresh coriander
4 tsps. minced garlic
1 tsp. ground cumin
1 tsp. chili powder

1. Brush the air fryer basket with olive oil.
2. Put the flank steak in a large mixing bowl. Season with salt and pepper.
3. Add the lime juice, coriander, garlic, cumin, and chili powder and toss to coat the steak.
4. For the best flavour, let the steak marinate in the refrigerator for about 1 hour.
5. Preheat the air fryer to 205ºC
6. Put the steak in the air fryer basket. Air fry for 7 minutes. Flip the steak. Air fry for 7 minutes more or until an internal temperature reaches at least 65ºC.
7. Let the steak rest for about 5 minutes, then cut into strips to serve.

Sun-dried Tomato Crusted Chops

Prep time: 15 minutes | Cook time: 10 minutes | Serves 4

27 g oil-packed sun-dried tomatoes
65 g toasted almonds
22 g grated Parmesan cheese
120 ml olive oil, plus more for brushing the air
fryer basket
2 tbsps. water
½ tsp. salt
Freshly ground black pepper, to taste
4 centre-cut boneless pork chops (567 g)

1. Put the sun-dried tomatoes into a food processor and pulse them until they are coarsely chopped. Add the almonds, Parmesan cheese, olive oil, water, salt and pepper. Process into a smooth paste. Spread most of the paste (leave a little in reserve) onto both sides of the pork chops and then pierce the meat several times with a needle-style meat tenderizer or a fork. Let the pork chops sit and marinate for at least 1 hour (refrigerate if marinating for longer than

1 hour).
2. Preheat the air fryer to 190ºC.
3. Brush more olive oil on the bottom of the air fryer basket. Transfer the pork chops into the air fryer basket, spooning a little more of the sun-dried tomato paste onto the pork chops if there are any gaps where the paste may have been rubbed off. Air fry the pork chops for 10 minutes, turning the chops over halfway through.
4. When the pork chops have finished cooking, transfer them to a serving plate and serve.

Steak and Kidney Pie

Prep time: 15 minutes | Cook time: 1 hour | Serves 8

cooking spray
2 sheep's kidneys, washed, skinned, halved, core removed, cut into 1.25 cm cubes
500 g stewing steak (blade, flank, skirt or round), cut into 2.5 cm cubes
3 tbsps. plain flour
1 tsp. salt
freshly ground black pepper
2 tbsps. olive oil
120 ml water
2 tbsps. parsley, finely chopped
1 roll of puff pastry
1 egg, beaten

1. Preheat the air fryer to 220ºC and spray the air fryer basket with oil.
2. Put the flour and seasonings into a plastic bag and add the steak and kidney pieces, shaking to cover well.
3. Heat the oil in a heavy pan and brown the meat, stirring constantly for about 5 minutes.
4. Add the water, cover tightly, and simmer for at least one hour or until well cooked.
5. Cool and stir in the parsley. Roll out the pastry until it is slightly larger than the lid of the pie dish.
6. Cut a strip about 2.5 cm wide and place it around the dampened rim of the dish. Brush with cold water and spoon the steak and kidney mixture into the dish, then cover with the remaining pastry, pressing into the pastry rim to seal.
7. With thumb or knife end press a pattern around the edge of the pie and glaze with the egg, making a hole in the middle to allow the steam to escape. Place in the basket and bake for 18 minutes, then reduce the heat to 180°C and cook for a further 25 minutes or until the pastry is golden.

BBQ Pork Steaks

Prep time: 5 minutes | Cook time: 15 minutes | Serves 4

4 pork steaks	1 tsp. soy sauce
1 tbsp. Cajun seasoning	110 g brown sugar
2 tbsps. BBQ sauce	117 g ketchup
1 tbsp. vinegar	

1. Preheat the air fryer to 140ºC.
2. Sprinkle pork steaks with Cajun seasoning.
3. Combine remaining ingredients and brush onto steaks.
4. Add coated steaks to air fryer. Air fry 15 minutes until just browned.
5. Serve immediately.

Sunday Roast

Prep time: 30 minutes | Cook time: 1 hour 30 minutes | Serves 4

cooking spray	1 large egg
For The Potatoes:	75 ml milk
900 g potatoes, peeled and cut into bite-size chunks	4 tsps. sunflower oil
	For The Gravy:
2 tbsps. sunflower oil	100 ml red wine
2 garlic bulbs, halved widthways	1 tbsp. brown sugar
	300 ml beef stock
For The Beef:	1 tbsp. cornflour
900 g beef roasting joint	**For The Vegetables:**
For The Yorkshire Puddings:	200 g Chantenay carrots
	400 g savoy cabbage, core removed, sliced
75 g plain flour	50 g butter

1. Preheat the air fryer to 180ºC and spay the air fryer basket with oil. Put the potatoes in a pan of salted water and bring to the boil. Parboil for 5 minutes, then drain.
2. In a skillet, heat the oil. Add the potatoes and garlic halves to the hot oil – turning them to coat. Place in the basket and air fry for 12 minutes.
3. Reduce the air fryer's temperature to 160˚C. Remove the potatoes and set aside, keeping warm. Season the beef joint and place in the air fryer basket.
4. Roast the beef for about 45 minutes for medium-rare, basting every 15 minutes.
5. Meanwhile, prepare the Yorkshire pudding batter. Sift the flour into a bowl and season with black pepper. In a jug, whisk together the egg, milk and 50 ml water. Make a well in the flour and gradually pour in the egg mix, whisking until smooth. Set aside.
6. To make the gravy, put the wine and sugar in a small saucepan and simmer for 2-3 minutes. Add the stock and continue to reduce by a third. Whisk together the cornflour and 1 tbsp. water in a small cup, then stir it into the gravy to thicken.
7. When the beef is cooked, remove from the air fryer and cover loosely with foil. Let it rest for a minimum of 15 minutes.
8. Meanwhile, increase the air fryer to 200˚C. Spray the 8 holes of a fairy cake or muffin tin with the oil, then remove and carefully divide the Yorkshire pudding batter between each. Bake for 8-10 minutes until the Yorkshires are golden, risen and crisp.
9. Meanwhile, parboil the carrots for 8-10 minutes until tender. Blanch the cabbage in boiling water for 2 minutes. Drain the vegetables and stir through the butter. Reheat the gravy over a medium-low heat if needed.
10. Use a sharp knife to carve the beef into thin slices and arrange on warm serving plates. Serve the beef with the potatoes, Yorkshire puddings, carrots, cabbage and gravy.

Beef Chuck with Brussels Sprouts

Prep time: 20 minutes | Cook time: 15 minutes | Serves 4

454 g beef chuck shoulder steak	1 tsp. onion powder
	½ tsp. garlic powder
2 tbsps. vegetable oil	227 g Brussels sprouts, cleaned and halved
1 tbsp. red wine vinegar	
1 tsp. fine sea salt	½ tsp. fennel seeds
½ tsp. ground black pepper	1 tsp. dried basil
	1 tsp. dried sage
1 tsp. smoked paprika	

1. Massage the beef with the vegetable oil, wine vinegar, salt, black pepper, paprika, onion powder, and garlic powder, coating it well.
2. Allow to marinate for a minimum of 3 hours.
3. Preheat the air fryer to 200ºC.
4. Remove the beef from the marinade and put in the preheated air fryer. Air fry for 10 minutes. Flip the beef halfway through.
5. Put the prepared Brussels sprouts in the air fryer along with the fennel seeds, basil, and sage.
6. Lower the heat to 190ºC and air fry everything for another 5 minutes.
7. Give them a good stir. Air fry for an additional 10 minutes.
8. Serve immediately.

Bacon Wrapped Pork with Apple Gravy

Prep time: 10 minutes | Cook time: 25 minutes | Serves 4

Pork:
1 tbsp.Dijon mustard
1 pork tenderloin
3 strips bacon
Apple Gravy:
3 tbsps. ghee, divided

1 small shallot, chopped
2 apples
1 tbsp. almond flour
240 ml vegetable stock
½ tsp. Dijon mustard

1. Preheat the air fryer to 180ºC.
2. Spread Dijon mustard all over tenderloin and wrap with strips of bacon.
3. Put into air fryer and air fry for 12 minutes. Use a meat thermometer to check for doneness.
4. To make sauce, heat 1 tbsp.of ghee in a pan and add shallots. Cook for 1 minute.
5. Then add apples, cooking for 4 minutes until softened.
6. Add flour and 2 tbsps. of ghee to make a roux. Add stock and mustard, stirring well to combine.
7. When sauce starts to bubble, add 1 cup of sautéed apples, cooking until sauce thickens.
8. Once pork tenderloin is cooked, allow to sit 8 minutes to rest before slicing.
9. Serve topped with apple gravy.

Shepard's Pie

Prep time: 20 minutes | Cook time: 45 minutes | Serves 5

2 onions (peeled and diced)
2 large carrots (peeled and diced)
2 tbsps. olive oil
50 g butter
sprigs thyme
500 g minced lamb
1 tbsp. tomato puree
1 tbsp. ketchup

2 tbsps. Worcestershire sauce
1 L beef or chicken stock
250 g frozen peas
500 g (to 600) potatoes (peeled and cut into chunks)
120 ml milk
100 g butter
2 egg yolks

1. Preheat the air fryer to 190ºC.
2. Sauté the onions and carrots with the olive oil and butter in a skillet, until just staring to colour. Add the thyme and beef.
3. Turn up the heat and brown the beef.
4. Add in remaining ingredients up until the stock.
5. Cook for 20 minutes until the liquid has reduced.

6. Season and allow to cool down.
7. Add the peas and then transfer to the air fryer basket.
8. Cook the potatoes until tender and milk with the remaining ingredients.
9. Top the meat mixture and spread the potatoes on top.
10. Bake in the air fryer until the topping is golden brown.
11. Allow to rest for 10 minutes before serving.

Beef Wellington

Prep time: 10 minutes | Cook time: 35 minutes | Serves 6

cooking spray
1 kg fillet of beef, well-trimmed
1 tbsp. olive oil
75 g butter
1 small onion, finely chopped
2 shallots, finely chopped

350 g mushrooms, finely chopped
Salt and ground black pepper
A pinch nutmeg
500 g roll of ready-made puff pastry,
1 egg, beaten

1. Preheat the air fryer to 230ºC and spay the air fryer basket with oil.
2. Heat the oil and 50 g of the butter in a small pan, add the onion and shallots and cook until transparent.
3. Add the mushrooms, seasoning and nutmeg. Stir over a moderate heat until all moisture from the mushrooms has evaporated. Transfer to a plate to cool.
4. Heat the remaining butter in a frying pan. Season the beef then brown it on all sides. This should take about five minutes. Allow to cool while you roll the pastry into an oblong shape, large enough to wrap around the beef.
5. Spread the cold mushroom mixture over the pastry, leaving a 2cm border all around. Moisten the edges with beaten egg. Place the cooled meat in the centre and wrap the pastry around it. Seal the edges and place on the basket, with the seal underneath. Use the pasty trimmings to make leaves for decoration, brush with a little egg and place on top of the parcel. Brush the parcel with the rest of the beaten egg.
6. Chill in the fridge for 20 minutes to allow the pastry to rest before baking.
7. Bake for 10 minutes. Then turn the temperature down to 200°C for a further 22 minutes. The beef will be medium rare at this stage. Cook for five minutes less is you like it rare.

Super Bacon with Meat

Prep time: 5 minutes | Cook time: 1 hour | Serves 4

30 slices thick-cut bacon
113 g Cheddar cheese, shredded
340 g steak
283 g pork sausage
Salt and ground black pepper, to taste

1. Preheat the air fryer to 200ºC.
2. Lay out 30 slices of bacon in a woven pattern and bake for 20 minutes until crisp. Put the cheese in the centre of the bacon.
3. Combine the steak and sausage to form a meaty mixture.
4. Lay out the meat in a rectangle of similar size to the bacon strips. Season with salt and pepper.
5. Roll the meat into a tight roll and refrigerate.
6. Preheat the air fryer to 200ºC.
7. Make a 7×7 bacon weave and roll the bacon weave over the meat, diagonally.
8. Bake for 60 minutes or until the internal temperature reaches at least 75ºC.
9. Let rest for 5 minutes before serving.

Beef Egg Rolls

Prep time: 15 minutes | Cook time: 12 minutes | Makes 8 egg rolls

½ chopped onion
2 garlic cloves, chopped
½ packet taco seasoning
Salt and ground black pepper, to taste
454 g lean beef mince
½ can coriander lime
rotel
16 egg roll wrappers
85 g shredded Mexican cheese
1 tbsp. olive oil
1 tsp. coriander

1. Preheat the air fryer to 200ºC.
2. Add onions and garlic to a skillet, cooking until fragrant. Then add taco seasoning, pepper, salt, and beef, cooking until beef is broke up into tiny pieces and cooked thoroughly.
3. Add rotel and stir well.
4. Lay out egg wrappers and brush with a touch of water to soften a bit.
5. Load wrappers with beef filling and add cheese to each.
6. Fold diagonally to close and use water to secure edges.
7. Brush filled egg wrappers with olive oil and add to the air fryer.
8. Air fry 8 minutes, flip, and air fry for another 4 minutes.

9. Serve sprinkled with coriander.

Bacon and Pear Stuffed Pork Chops

Prep time: 20 minutes | Cook time: 24 minutes | Serves 3

4 slices bacon, chopped
1 tbsp. butter
25 g finely diced onion
80 ml chicken stock
150 g seasoned stuffing cubes
1 egg, beaten
½ tsp. dried thyme
½ tsp. salt
⅛ tsp. freshly ground
black pepper
1 pear, finely diced
75 g crumbled blue cheese
3 boneless centre-cut pork chops (4-cm thick)
Olive oil, for greasing
Salt and freshly ground black pepper, to taste

1. Preheat the air fryer to 200ºC.
2. Put the bacon into the air fryer basket and air fry for 6 minutes, stirring halfway through the cooking time. Remove the bacon and set it aside on a paper towel. Pour out the grease from the bottom of the air fryer.
3. To make the stuffing, melt the butter in a medium saucepan over medium heat on the stovetop. Add the onion and sauté for a few minutes until it starts to soften. Add the chicken stock and simmer for 1 minute. Remove the pan from the heat and add the stuffing cubes. Stir until the stock has been absorbed. Add the egg, dried thyme, salt and freshly ground black pepper, and stir until combined. Fold in the diced pear and crumbled blue cheese.
4. Put the pork chops on a cutting board. Using the palm of the hand to hold the chop flat and steady, slice into the side of the pork chop to make a pocket in the centre of the chop. Leave about 2-cm of chop uncut and make sure you don't cut all the way through the pork chop. Brush both sides of the pork chops with olive oil and season with salt and freshly ground black pepper. Stuff each pork chop with a third of the stuffing, packing the stuffing tightly inside the pocket.
5. Preheat the air fryer to 180ºC.
6. Spray or brush the sides of the air fryer basket with oil. Put the pork chops in the air fryer basket with the open, stuffed edge of the pork chop facing the outside edges of the basket.
7. Air fry the pork chops for 18 minutes, turning the pork chops over halfway through the cooking time. When the chops are done, let them rest for 5 minutes and then transfer to a serving platter.

Roast Beef

Prep time: <5 minutes | Cook time: 1 hour-1 hour 20 minutes | Serves 5-6

cooking spray
900 g beef roasting joint
2 carrots, diced
2 onions, diced

1. Preheat the air fryer to 180ºC and spay the air fryer basket with oil.
2. Put the diced carrots and onions in the air fryer basket.
3. Place the beef joint on top of the vegetables.
4. Season the beef and cover loosely with tinfoil.
5. Air fry for 1 hour 20 minutes depending on how you like your beef cooked.

Cottage Pie

Prep time: <5 minutes | Cook time: 45 minutes | Serves 4-5

cooking spray
450 g minced beef
1 tin of chopped tomatoes
1 medium onion, chopped
2 carrot, medium peeled and diced
100 g frozen peas
2 garlic cloves
Veg, chicken or beef stock cube
Gravy granules (enough to thicken)
600 ml water
Potatoes (Not white) – 8 medium potatoes
25 g butter
50 ml milk or cream
Salt and pepper to taste

1. Preheat the air fryer to 180ºC and spray the air fryer basket with oil.
2. Peel and chop the onion, garlic and carrots then heat the pan or pot with about 2 tbsps. of oil.
3. Add the veg you just chopped to the pan and cook slowly without colouring until the onions are soft.
4. Peel the potatoes then make sure they are roughly the same size, add to the other pot then cover with cold water
5. Place on high heat until boiling then turn the heat down, cover with a lid and simmer till cooked. Test with a fork, if it easily goes through a potato then they are cooked.
6. Add the mince and use a wooden or metal spoon to break it apart so there are no lumps, you want to cook it until it has browned.
7. Add the chopped tomatoes and stir well then add the water and stock cube, stir then turn the heat right down and allow to simmer for 15 minutes, if you leave it longer you may need to add more water.
8. Add the peas and cook for a further 5 or so minutes.
9. Add 2 tbsps. gravy granules to the pan then stir well, you may need to add more as the dish shouldn't be watery at all.
10. Pour the mince sauce into the air fryer basket, don't overfill or it will overflow when you add the mash.
11. Mash the potatoes then add the butter and milk or cream with ½ tsp. each of salt and pepper.
12. Spoon the mash on top of the mince mix in the basket then bake at 180ºC for 22 minutes.

Kale and Beef Omelet

Prep time: 15 minutes | Cook time: 16 minutes | Serves 4

227 g leftover beef, coarsely chopped
2 garlic cloves, pressed
40 g kale, torn into pieces and wilted
1 tomato, chopped
¼ tsp. sugar
4 eggs, beaten
4 tbsps. heavy cream
½ tsp. turmeric powder
Salt and ground black pepper, to taste
⅛ tsp. ground allspice
Cooking spray

1. Preheat the air fryer to 180ºC. Spritz four ramekins with cooking spray.
2. Put equal amounts of each of the ingredients into each ramekin and mix well.
3. Air fry for 16 minutes. Serve immediately.

Beef and Spinach Rolls

Prep time: 10 minutes | Cook time: 14 minutes | Serves 2

3 tsps. pesto
907 g beef flank steak
6 slices provolone cheese
85 g roasted red peppers
30 g baby spinach
1 tsp. sea salt
1 tsp. black pepper

1. Preheat the air fryer to 200ºC.
2. Spoon equal amounts of the pesto onto each flank steak and spread it across evenly.
3. Put the cheese, roasted red peppers and spinach on top of the meat, about three-quarters of the way down.
4. Roll the steak up, holding it in place with toothpicks. Sprinkle with the sea salt and pepper.
5. Put inside the air fryer and air fry for 14 minutes, turning halfway through the cooking time.
6. Allow the beef to rest for 10 minutes before slicing up and serving.

Spinach and Beef Braciole

Prep time: 25 minutes | Cook time: 1 hour 32 minutes | Serves 4

½ onion, finely chopped
1 tsp. olive oil
80 ml red wine
300 g crushed tomatoes
1 tsp. Italian seasoning
½ tsp. garlic powder
¼ tsp. crushed red pepper flakes
2 tbsps. chopped fresh parsley
2 top round steaks (680 g)
salt and freshly ground black pepper
80 g fresh spinach, chopped
1 clove minced garlic
75 g roasted red peppers, julienned
40 g grated pecorino cheese
37 g pine nuts, toasted and roughly chopped
2 tbsps. olive oil

1. Preheat the air fryer to 200ºC.
2. Toss the onions and olive oil together in a casserole dish. Air fry at 204ºC for 5 minutes, stirring a couple times during the cooking process. Add the red wine, crushed tomatoes, Italian seasoning, garlic powder, red pepper flakes and parsley and stir. Cover the dish tightly with aluminum foil, lower the air fryer temperature to 180ºC and continue to air fry for 15 minutes.
3. While the sauce is simmering, prepare the beef. Using a meat mallet, pound the beef until it is ½- cm thick. Season both sides of the beef with salt and pepper. Combine the spinach, garlic, red peppers, pecorino cheese, pine nuts and olive oil in a medium bowl. Season with salt and freshly ground black pepper. Disperse the mixture over the steaks. Starting at one of the short ends, roll the beef around the filling, tucking in the sides as you roll to ensure the filling is completely enclosed. Secure the beef rolls with toothpicks.
4. Remove the casserole dish with the sauce from the air fryer and set it aside. Preheat the air fryer to 200ºC.
5. Brush or spray the beef rolls with a little olive oil and air fry at 200ºC for 12 minutes, rotating the beef during the cooking process for even browning. When the beef is browned, submerge the rolls into the sauce in the casserole dish, cover the pan with foil and return it to the air fryer. Reduce the temperature of the air fryer to 120ºC and air fry for 60 minutes.
6. Remove the beef rolls from the sauce. Cut each roll into slices and serve, ladling some sauce overtop.

Lancashire Hotpot

Prep time: 20 minutes | Cook time: 2 hours 30 minutes | Serves 4

900 g boneless lamb rib or shoulder, cut into 4-cm pieces
Salt and black pepper
1 tsp. dried thyme
2 bay leaves
2 large onions, peeled
and sliced
680 g potatoes, peeled and sliced
350 ml lamb or vegetable stock
Sunflower oil or melted butter, for glazing

1. Preheat the air fryer to 170ºC.
2. Place the lamb in a large ovenproof casserole dish.
3. Season with salt and pepper, sprinkle over the thyme and bay leaves. Add the onions, then arrange the potatoes on top in overlapping layers.
4. Slowly pour the stock into the dish. Brush the top of the potatoes with oil or butter. Cover and bake in the air fryer for 2 hours, or until the meat is tender.
5. Increase the air fryer temperature to 200°C. And bake for another 30 minutes, or until the potatoes are golden.

Cheddar Bacon Burst with Spinach

Prep time: 5 minutes | Cook time: 60 minutes | Serves 8

30 slices bacon
1 tbsp. Chipotle seasoning
2 tsps. Italian seasoning
208 g Cheddar cheese
120 g raw spinach

1. Preheat the air fryer to 190ºC.
2. Weave the bacon into 15 vertical pieces and 12 horizontal pieces. Cut the extra 3 in half to fill in the rest, horizontally.
3. Season the bacon with Chipotle seasoning and Italian seasoning.
4. Add the cheese to the bacon.
5. Add the spinach and press down to compress.
6. Tightly roll up the woven bacon.
7. Line a baking sheet with kitchen foil and add plenty of salt to it.
8. Put the bacon on top of a cooling rack and put that on top of the baking sheet.
9. Bake for 60 minutes.
10. Let cool for 15 minutes before slicing and serve.

Peppercorn Crusted Beef Tenderloin

Prep time: 5 minutes | Cook time: 25 minutes | Serves 6

907 g beef tenderloin
2 tsps. roasted garlic, minced
2 tbsps. salted butter,

melted
3 tbsps. ground 4-peppercorn blender

1. Preheat the air fryer to 200ºC.
2. Remove any surplus fat from the beef tenderloin.
3. Combine the roasted garlic and melted butter to apply to the tenderloin with a brush.
4. On a plate, spread out the peppercorns and roll the tenderloin in them, making sure they are covering and clinging to the meat.
5. Air fry the tenderloin in the air fryer for 25 minutes, turning halfway through cooking.
6. Let the tenderloin rest for ten minutes before slicing and serving.

Beef and Cheddar Burgers

Prep time: 20 minutes | Cook time: 25 minutes | Serves 4

1 tbsp. olive oil
1 onion, sliced into rings
1 tsp. garlic, minced or puréed
1 tsp. mustard
1 tsp. basil
1 tsp. mixed herbs
Salt and ground black

pepper, to taste
1 tsp. tomato, puréed
4 buns
28 g Cheddar cheese, sliced
298 g beef, minced
Salad leaves

1. Preheat the air fryer to 200ºC.
2. Grease the air fryer with olive oil and allow it to warm up.
3. Put the minced beef in the air fryer and air fry until they turn golden brown.
4. Mix in the garlic, mustard, basil, herbs, salt, and pepper, and air fry for 25 minutes.
5. Lay 2 to 3 onion rings and puréed tomato on two of the buns. Put one slice of cheese and the layer of beef on top. Top with salad leaves before closing off the sandwich with the other buns.
6. Serve immediately.

Pork Chops with Rinds

Prep time: 5 minutes | Cook time: 15 minutes | Serves 4

1 tsp. chili powder
½ tsp. garlic powder
43 g pork rinds, finely ground

4 (113-g) pork chops
1 tbsp. coconut oil, melted

1. Preheat the air fryer to 200ºC.
2. Combine the chili powder, garlic powder, and ground pork rinds.
3. Coat the pork chops with the coconut oil, followed by the pork rind mixture, taking care to cover them completely. Then place the chops in the air fryer basket.
4. Air fry the chops for 15 minutes or until the internal temperature of the chops reaches at least 65ºC, turning halfway through.
5. Serve immediately.

Beef Cheeseburger Egg Rolls

Prep time: 15 minutes | Cook time: 8 minutes | Makes 6 egg rolls

227 g raw lean beef mince
20 g chopped onion
60 g chopped pepper
¼ tsp. onion powder
¼ tsp. garlic powder
3 tbsps. cream cheese

1 tbsp. yellow mustard
3 tbsps. shredded Cheddar cheese
6 chopped dill pickle chips
6 egg roll wrappers

1. Preheat the air fryer to 200ºC.
2. In a skillet, add the beef, onion, pepper, onion powder, and garlic powder. Stir and crumble beef until fully cooked, and vegetables are soft.
3. Take skillet off the heat and add cream cheese, mustard, and Cheddar cheese, stirring until melted.
4. Pour beef mixture into a bowl and fold in pickles.
5. Lay out egg wrappers and divide the beef mixture into each one. Moisten egg roll wrapper edges with water. Fold sides to the middle and seal with water.
6. Repeat with all other egg rolls.
7. Put rolls into air fryer, one batch at a time. Air fry for 8 minutes.
8. Serve immediately.

Chapter 7 Poultry

Tex-Mex Turkey Burgers

Prep time: 10 minutes | Cook time: 14 to 16 minutes | Serves 4

15 g finely crushed corn tortilla chips	Pinch salt
1 egg, beaten	Freshly ground black pepper, to taste
60 g salsa	454 g turkey mince
30 g shredded pepper Jack cheese	1 tbsp. olive oil
	1 tsp. paprika

1. Preheat the air fryer to 170ºC.
2. In a medium bowl, combine the tortilla chips, egg, salsa, cheese, salt, and pepper, and mix well.
3. Add the turkey and mix gently but thoroughly with clean hands.
4. Form the meat mixture into patties about 1-cm thick. Make an indentation in the centre of each patty with your thumb so the burgers don't puff up while cooking.
5. Brush the patties on both sides with the olive oil and sprinkle with paprika.
6. Put in the air fryer basket and air fry for 14 to 16 minutes or until the meat registers at least 75ºC.
7. Let sit for 5 minutes before serving.

Tempero Baiano Brazilian Chicken

Prep time: 5 minutes | Cook time: 20 minutes | Serves 4

1 tsp. cumin seeds	½ tsp. black peppercorns
1 tsp. dried oregano	½ tsp. cayenne pepper
1 tsp. dried parsley	60 ml fresh lime juice
1 tsp. ground turmeric	2 tbsps. olive oil
½ tsp. coriander seeds	680 g chicken drumsticks
1 tsp. salt	

1. In a clean coffee grinder or spice mill, combine the cumin, oregano, parsley, turmeric, coriander seeds, salt, peppercorns, and cayenne. Process until finely ground.
2. In a small bowl, combine the ground spices with the lime juice and oil. Place the chicken in a resealable plastic bag. Add the marinade, seal, and massage until the chicken is well coated. Marinate at room temperature for 30 minutes or in the refrigerator for

up to 24 hours.
3. Preheat the air fryer to 200ºC.
4. Place the drumsticks skin-side up in the air fryer basket and air fry for 20 to 25 minutes, turning the drumsticks halfway through the cooking time. Use a meat thermometer to ensure that the chicken has reached an internal temperature of 75ºC. Serve immediately.

Orange and Honey Glazed Duck with Apples

Prep time: 5 minutes | Cook time: 15 minutes | Serves 2 to 3

454 g duck breasts (2 to 3 breasts)	85 g honey
	2 sprigs thyme, plus more for garnish
Salt and pepper, to taste	2 firm tart apples, such as Fuji
Juice and zest of 1 orange	

1. Preheat the air fryer to 200ºC.
2. Pat the duck breasts dry and, using a sharp knife, make 3 to 4 shallow, diagonal slashes in the skin. Turn the breasts and score the skin on the diagonal in the opposite direction to create a cross-hatch pattern. Season well with salt and pepper.
3. Place the duck breasts skin-side up in the air fryer basket. Roast for 8 minutes, then flip and roast for 4 more minutes on the second side.
4. While the duck is cooking, prepare the sauce. Combine the orange juice and zest, honey, and thyme in a small saucepan. Bring to a boil, stirring to dissolve the honey, then reduce the heat and simmer until thickened. Core the apples and cut into quarters. Cut each quarter into 3 or 4 slices depending on the size.
5. After the duck has cooked on both sides, turn it and brush the skin with the orange-honey glaze. Roast for 1 more minute. Remove the duck breasts to a cutting board and allow to rest.
6. Toss the apple slices with the remaining orange-honey sauce in a medium bowl. Arrange the apples in a single layer in the air fryer basket. Air fry for 10 minutes while the duck breast rests. Slice the duck breasts on the bias and divide them and the apples among 2 or 3 plates.
7. Serve warm, garnished with additional thyme.

Turkey, Hummus, and Cheese Wraps

Prep time: 10 minutes | Cook time: 3 to 4 minutes | Serves 4

4 large whole wheat wraps
120 g hummus
16 thin slices deli turkey
8 slices provolone cheese
40 g fresh baby spinach, or more to taste

1. Preheat the air fryer to 180ºC.
2. To assemble, place 2 tbsps. of hummus on each wrap and spread to within about a 1-cm from edges. Top with 4 slices of turkey and 2 slices of provolone. Finish with baby spinach, or pile on as much as you like.
3. Roll up each wrap. You don't need to fold or seal the ends.
4. Place 2 wraps in air fryer basket, seam-side down.
5. Air fry for 3 to 4 minutes to warm filling and melt cheese. Repeat step 4 to air fry the remaining wraps. Serve immediately.

Pecan-Crusted Turkey Cutlets

Prep time: 10 minutes | Cook time: 10 to 12 minutes | Serves 4

90 g panko bread crumbs
¼ tsp. salt
¼ tsp. pepper
¼ tsp. dry mustard
¼ tsp. poultry seasoning
75 g pecans
30 g cornflour
1 egg, beaten
454 g turkey cutlets, 1-cm thick
Salt and pepper, to taste
Cooking spray

1. Preheat the air fryer to 180ºC.
2. Place the panko crumbs, salt, pepper, mustard, and poultry seasoning in a food processor. Process until crumbs are finely crushed. Add pecans and process just until nuts are finely chopped.
3. Place cornflour in a shallow dish and beaten egg in another. Transfer coating mixture from food processor into a third shallow dish.
4. Sprinkle turkey cutlets with salt and pepper to taste.
5. Dip cutlets in cornflour and shake off excess, then dip in beaten egg and finally roll in crumbs, pressing to coat well. Spray both sides with cooking spray.
6. Place 2 cutlets in air fryer basket in a single layer and air fry for 10 to 12 minutes. Repeat with the remaining cutlets.
7. Serve warm.

Easy Asian Turkey Meatballs

Prep time: 10 minutes | Cook time: 11 to 14 minutes | Serves 4

2 tbsps. peanut oil, divided
1 small onion, minced
30 g water chestnuts, finely chopped
½ tsp. ground ginger
2 tbsps. low-sodium soy sauce
60 g panko bread crumbs
1 egg, beaten
454 g turkey mince

1. Preheat the air fryer to 200ºC.
2. In a round metal pan, combine 1 tbsp. of peanut oil and onion. Air fry for 1 to 2 minutes or until crisp and tender. Transfer the onion to a medium bowl.
3. Add the water chestnuts, ground ginger, soy sauce, and bread crumbs to the onion and mix well. Add egg and stir well. Mix in the turkey mince until combined.
4. Form the mixture into 2-cm meatballs. Drizzle the remaining 1 tbsp. of oil over the meatballs.
5. Bake the meatballs in the pan in batches for 10 to 12 minutes or until they are 75ºC on a meat thermometer. Rest for 5 minutes before serving.

Apricot Glazed Turkey Tenderloin

Prep time: 20 minutes | Cook time: 30 minutes | Serves 4

80 g sugar-free apricot preserves
½ tbsp. spicy brown mustard
680 g turkey breast
tenderloin
Salt and freshly ground black pepper, to taste
Olive oil spray

1. Preheat the air fryer to 188ºC. Spray the air fryer basket lightly with olive oil spray.
2. In a small bowl, combine the apricot preserves and mustard to make a paste.
3. Season the turkey with salt and pepper. Spread the apricot paste all over the turkey.
4. Place the turkey in the air fryer basket and lightly spray with olive oil spray.
5. Air fry for 15 minutes. Flip the turkey over and lightly spray with olive oil spray. Air fry until the internal temperature reaches at least 80ºC, an additional 10 to 15 minutes.
6. Let the turkey rest for 10 minutes before slicing and serving.

Mayonnaise-Mustard Chicken

Prep time: 10 minutes | Cook time: 15 minutes | Serves 4

6 tbsps. mayonnaise	2 tsps. curry powder
2 tbsps. coarse-ground mustard	1 tsp. salt
2 tsps. honey (optional)	1 tsp. cayenne pepper
	454 g chicken tenders

1. Preheat the air fryer to 180ºC.
2. In a large bowl, whisk together the mayonnaise, mustard, honey (if using), curry powder, salt, and cayenne. Transfer half of the mixture to a serving bowl to serve as a dipping sauce. Add the chicken tenders to the large bowl and toss until well coated.
3. Place the tenders in the air fryer basket and bake for 15 minutes. Use a meat thermometer to ensure the chicken has reached an internal temperature of 75ºC.
4. Serve the chicken with the dipping sauce.

Sweet and Spicy Turkey Meatballs

Prep time: 15 minutes | Cook time: 15 minutes | Serves 6

454 g lean turkey mince	2 tsps. minced garlic
60 g whole-wheat panko bread crumbs	⅛ tsp. salt
1 egg, beaten	⅛ tsp. freshly ground black pepper
1 tbsp. soy sauce	1 tsp. sriracha
60 ml plus 1 tbsp. hoisin sauce, divided	Olive oil spray

1. Preheat the air fryer to 180ºC. Spray the air fryer basket lightly with olive oil spray.
2. In a large bowl, mix together the turkey, panko bread crumbs, egg, soy sauce, 1 tbsp. of hoisin sauce, garlic, salt, and black pepper.
3. Using a tablespoon, form the mixture into 24 meatballs.
4. In a small bowl, combine the remaining 60 ml of hoisin sauce and sriracha to make a glaze and set aside.
5. Place the meatballs in the air fryer basket in a single layer. You may need to cook them in batches.
6. Air fry for 8 minutes. Brush the meatballs generously with the glaze and air fry until cooked through, an additional 4 to 7 minutes. Serve warm.

Air-Fried Chicken Wings

Prep time: 5 minutes | Cook time: 19 minutes | Serves 6

907 g chicken wings, tips removed	⅛ tsp. salt

1. Preheat the air fryer to 200ºC. Season the wings with salt.
2. Working in 2 batches, place half the chicken wings in the basket and air fry for 15 minutes, or until the skin is browned and cooked through, turning the wings with tongs halfway through cooking.
3. Combine both batches in the air fryer and air fry for 4 minutes more. Transfer to a large bowl and serve immediately.

Chicken-Lettuce Wraps

Prep time: 15 minutes | Cook time: 12 to 16 minutes | Serves 2 to 4

454 g boneless, skinless chicken thighs, trimmed	pieces
1 tsp. vegetable oil	25 g chopped fresh mint
2 tbsps. lime juice	25 g chopped fresh coriander
1 shallot, minced	25 g chopped fresh Thai basil
1 tbsp. fish sauce, plus extra for serving	1 head Bibb lettuce, leaves separated (227 g)
2 tsps. packed brown sugar	30 g chopped dry-roasted peanuts
1 garlic clove, minced	2 Thai chilies, stemmed and sliced thin
⅛ tsp. red pepper flakes	
1 mango, peeled, pitted, and cut into 1/2 –cm	

1. Preheat the air fryer to 205ºC.
2. Pat the chicken dry with paper towels and rub with oil. Place the chicken in air fryer basket and air fry for 12 to 16 minutes, or until the chicken registers 80ºC, flipping and rotating chicken halfway through cooking.
3. Meanwhile, whisk lime juice, shallot, fish sauce, sugar, garlic, and pepper flakes together in large bowl; set aside.
4. Transfer chicken to cutting board, let cool slightly, then shred into bite-size pieces using 2 forks. Add the shredded chicken, mango, mint, coriander, and basil to bowl with dressing and toss to coat.
5. Serve the chicken in the lettuce leaves, passing peanuts, Thai chilies, and extra fish sauce separately.

Turkey and Cranberry Quesadillas

Prep time: 7 minutes | Cook time: 4 to 8 minutes | Serves 4

6 low-sodium whole-wheat tortillas
30 g shredded low-sodium low-fat Swiss cheese
100 g shredded cooked

low-sodium turkey breast
2 tbsps. cranberry sauce
2 tbsps. dried cranberries
½ tsp. dried basil
Olive oil spray, for spraying the tortillas

1. Preheat the air fryer to 200ºC.
2. Put 3 tortillas on a work surface.
3. Evenly divide the Swiss cheese, turkey, cranberry sauce, and dried cranberries among the tortillas. Sprinkle with the basil and top with the remaining tortillas.
4. Spray the outsides of the tortillas with olive oil spray.
5. One at a time, air fry the quesadillas in the air fryer for 4 to 8 minutes, or until crisp and the cheese is melted. Cut into quarters and serve.

Herbed Turkey Breast

Prep time: 20 minutes | Cook time: 45 minutes | Serves 6

1 tbsp. olive oil
Cooking spray
2 garlic cloves, minced
2 tsps. Dijon mustard
1½ tsps. rosemary
1½ tsps. sage

1½ tsps. thyme
1 tsp. salt
½ tsp. freshly ground black pepper
1.4 kg turkey breast, thawed if frozen

1. Preheat the air fryer to 190ºC. Spray the air fryer basket lightly with cooking spray.
2. In a small bowl, mix together the garlic, olive oil, Dijon mustard, rosemary, sage, thyme, salt, and pepper to make a paste. Smear the paste all over the turkey breast.
3. Place the turkey breast in the air fryer basket. Air fry for 20 minutes. Flip turkey breast over and baste it with any drippings that have collected in the bottom drawer of the air fryer. Air fry until the internal temperature of the meat reaches at least 77ºC, 20 more minutes.
4. If desired, increase the temperature to 200ºC, flip the turkey breast over one last time, and air fry for 5 minutes to get a crispy exterior.
5. Let the turkey rest for 10 minutes before slicing and serving.

Roasted Cajun Turkey

Prep time: 10 minutes | Cook time: 30 minutes | Serves 4

907 g turkey thighs, skinless and boneless
1 red onion, sliced
2 peppers, sliced
1 habanero pepper, minced

1 carrot, sliced
1 tbsp. Cajun seasoning mix
1 tbsp. fish sauce
480 ml chicken stock
Nonstick cooking spray

1. Preheat the air fryer to 180ºC.
2. Spritz the bottom and sides of a baking dish with nonstick cooking spray.
3. Arrange the turkey thighs in the baking dish. Add the onion, peppers, and carrot. Sprinkle with Cajun seasoning. Add the fish sauce and chicken stock.
4. Roast in the preheated air fryer for 30 minutes until cooked through. Serve warm.

Ginger Chicken Thighs

Prep time: 10 minutes | Cook time: 10 minutes | Serves 4

15 g julienned peeled fresh ginger
2 tbsps. vegetable oil
1 tbsp. honey
1 tbsp. soy sauce
1 tbsp. ketchup
1 tsp. garam masala
1 tsp. ground turmeric

¼ tsp. salt
½ tsp. cayenne pepper
Vegetable oil spray
454 g boneless, skinless chicken thighs, cut crosswise into thirds
15 g chopped fresh coriander, for garnish

1. In a small bowl, combine the ginger, oil, honey, soy sauce, ketchup, garam masala, turmeric, salt, and cayenne. Whisk until well combined. Place the chicken in a resealable plastic bag and pour the marinade over. Seal the bag and massage to cover all of the chicken with the marinade. Marinate at room temperature for 30 minutes or in the refrigerator for up to 24 hours.
2. Preheat the air fryer to 180ºC.
3. Spray the air fryer basket with vegetable oil spray and add the chicken and as much of the marinade and julienned ginger as possible. Bake for 10 minutes. Use a meat thermometer to ensure the chicken has reached an internal temperature of 75ºC.
4. To serve, garnish with coriander.

Spiced Turkey Tenderloin

Prep time: 20 minutes | Cook time: 30 minutes | Serves 4

½ tsp. paprika
½ tsp. garlic powder
½ tsp. salt
½ tsp. freshly ground black pepper

Pinch cayenne pepper
680 g turkey breast tenderloin
Olive oil spray

1. Preheat the air fryer to 190ºC. Spray the air fryer basket lightly with olive oil spray.
2. In a small bowl, combine the paprika, garlic powder, salt, black pepper, and cayenne pepper. Rub the mixture all over the turkey.
3. Place the turkey in the air fryer basket and lightly spray with olive oil spray.
4. Air fry for 15 minutes. Flip the turkey over and lightly spray with olive oil spray. Air fry until the internal temperature reaches at least 80ºC for an additional 10 to 15 minutes.
5. Let the turkey rest for 10 minutes before slicing and serving.

Turkey Stuffed Peppers

Prep time: 20 minutes | Cook time: 15 minutes | Serves 4

227 g lean turkey mince
4 medium peppers
1 (425-g) can black beans, drained and rinsed
83 g shredded reduced-fat Cheddar cheese
250 g cooked long-grain brown rice
235 g mild salsa

1¼ tsps. chili powder
1 tsp. salt
½ tsp. ground cumin
½ tsp. freshly ground black pepper
Olive oil spray
Chopped fresh coriander, for garnish

1. Preheat the air fryer to 180ºC.
2. In a large skillet over medium-high heat, cook the turkey, breaking it up with a spoon, until browned, about 5 minutes. Drain off any excess fat.
3. Cut about 1-cm off the tops of the peppers and then cut in half lengthwise. Remove and discard the seeds and set the peppers aside.
4. In a large bowl, combine the browned turkey, black beans, Cheddar cheese, rice, salsa, chili powder, salt, cumin, and black pepper. Spoon the mixture into the peppers.
5. Lightly spray the air fryer basket with olive oil spray.
6. Place the stuffed peppers in the air fryer basket. Air fry until heated through, 10 to 15 minutes. Garnish with coriander and serve.

Chapter 8 Starters and Snacks

Rosemary Baked Cashews

Prep time: 5 minutes | Cook time: 3 minutes | Makes 2 cups

2 sprigs of fresh rosemary (1 chopped and 1 whole)
1 tsp. olive oil
1 tsp. salt
½ tsp. honey
300 g roasted and unsalted whole cashews
Cooking spray

1. Preheat the air fryer to 150ºC.
2. In a medium bowl, whisk together the chopped rosemary, olive oil, salt, and honey. Set aside.
3. Spray the air fryer basket with cooking spray, then place the cashews and the whole rosemary sprig in the basket and bake for 3 minutes.
4. Remove the cashews and rosemary from the air fryer, then discard the rosemary and add the cashews to the olive oil mixture, tossing to coat.
5. Allow to cool for 15 minutes before serving.

Artichoke-Spinach Dip

Prep time: 10 minutes | Cook time: 10 minutes | Makes 3 cups

1 (397-g) can artichoke hearts packed in water, drained and chopped
1 (284-g) package frozen spinach, thawed and drained
1 tsp. minced garlic
2 tbsps. mayonnaise
70 g nonfat plain Greek yogurt
56 g shredded low fat Mozzarella cheese
22 g grated Parmesan cheese
¼ tsp. freshly ground black pepper
Cooking spray

1. Preheat the air fryer to 180ºC.
2. Wrap the artichoke hearts and spinach in a paper towel and squeeze out any excess liquid, then transfer the vegetables to a large bowl.
3. Add the minced garlic, mayonnaise, plain Greek yogurt, Mozzarella, Parmesan, and black pepper to the large bowl, stirring well to combine.
4. Spray a baking dish with cooking spray, then transfer the dip mixture to the dish and air fry for 10 minutes.
5. Remove the dip from the air fryer and allow to cool on a wire rack for 10 minutes before serving.

Cayenne Sesame Nut Mix

Prep time: 10 minutes | Cook time: 2 minutes | Makes 4 cups

1 tbsp. buttery spread, melted
2 tsps. honey
¼ tsp. cayenne pepper
2 tsps. sesame seeds
¼ tsp. salt
¼ tsp. freshly ground
black pepper
150 g cashews
150 g almonds
90 g mini pretzels
40 g rice squares cereal
Cooking spray

1. Preheat the air fryer to 180ºC.
2. In a large bowl, combine the buttery spread, honey, cayenne pepper, sesame seeds, salt, and black pepper, then add the cashews, almonds, pretzels, and rice squares, tossing to coat.
3. Spray the air fryer basket with cooking spray, then pour the mixture into the pan and bake for 2 minutes.
4. Remove the sesame mix from the air fryer and allow to cool on a wire rack for 5 minutes before serving.

Root Veggie Chips with Herb Salt

Prep time: 10 minutes | Cook time: 8 minutes | Serves 2

1 parsnip, washed
1 small beetroot, washed
1 small turnip, washed
½ small sweet potato, washed
1 tsp. olive oil
Cooking spray
Herb Salt:
¼ tsp. salt
2 tsps. finely chopped fresh parsley

1. Preheat the air fryer to 180ºC.
2. Peel and thinly slice the parsnip, beetroot, turnip, and sweet potato, then place the vegetables in a large bowl, add the olive oil, and toss.
3. Spray the air fryer basket with cooking spray, then place the vegetables in the basket and air fry for 8 minutes, gently shaking the basket halfway through.
4. While the chips cook, make the herb salt in a small bowl by combining the salt and parsley.
5. Remove the chips and place on a serving plate, then sprinkle the herb salt on top and allow to cool for 2 to 3 minutes before serving.

Bacon-Wrapped Dates

Prep time: 10 minutes | Cook time: 10 to 14 minutes | Serves 6

12 dates, pitted
6 slices high-quality

bacon, cut in half
Cooking spray

1. Preheat the air fryer to 180ºC.
2. Wrap each date with half a bacon slice and secure with a toothpick.
3. Spray the air fryer basket with cooking spray, then place 6 bacon-wrapped dates in the basket and bake for 5 to 7 minutes or until the bacon is crispy. Repeat this process with the remaining dates.
4. Remove the dates and allow to cool on a wire rack for 5 minutes before serving.

Cornish Pasty

Prep time: 20 minutes | Cook time: 45 minutes | Serves 6

cooking spray
1 roll of ready-made
shortcrust pastry
For The Cornish Pasty Filling:
450 g potato, finely diced
150 g turnip, finely diced
150 g onion, finely

chopped
300 g beef skirt, finely chopped
Salt and black pepper
1 tbsp. plain flour
40 g butter
1 egg, beaten

1. Preheat the air fryer to 180ºC and spay the basket with oil.
2. Roll out the pastry.
3. Cut out 6 discs of pastry.
4. Season the vegetables separately with salt and black pepper.
5. Put the beef into a bowl and mix with the flour and some salt and pepper. Place some potatoes, turnip, onions, and beef on one half of the circle, leaving a gap around the edge. Dot with butter.
6. Brush around the perimeter of the pastry circle with the beaten egg, then fold the pastry over the vegetables and meat and seal firmly. Starting at one side, crimp the edges over to form a sealed D-shaped pasty.
7. Brush the whole pasty with a beaten egg, then make a steam hole in the center with a sharp knife.
8. Repeat to make the other pasties.
9. Put the pasties in the air fryer basket and bake for 45 minutes until they are crispy and golden and the filling is cooked through.
10. Leave them to rest for 5-10 minutes before eating.

Air Fried Baby Back Ribs

Prep time: 5 minutes | Cook time: 30 minutes | Serves 2

2 tsps. red pepper flakes
¾ tsp ground ginger
3 cloves minced garlic

Salt and ground black pepper, to taste
2 baby back ribs

1. Preheat the air fryer to 180ºC.
2. Combine the red pepper flakes, ginger, garlic, salt and pepper in a bowl, making sure to mix well. Massage the mixture into the baby back ribs.
3. Air fry the ribs in the air fryer for 30 minutes.
4. Take care when taking the rubs out of the air fryer. Put them on a serving dish and serve.

Toad in the Hole

Prep time: <5 minutes | Cook time: 50 minutes | Serves 12

cooking spray
For The Batter:
100 g plain flour
2 eggs
150 ml semi-skimmed milk
For The Toad:
8 pork sausages
1 onion, finely sliced
1 tbsp. vegetable oil

For The Gravy:
1 onion, finely sliced
1 tbsp. vegetable oil
2 tsps. plain flour
2 tsps. English mustard
2 tsps. Worcestershire sauce
1 vegetable stock cube, made up to 300ml

1. Preheat the air fryer to 200ºC and spay the air fryer basket with oil.
2. First make the batter. Put the flour in a bowl, add the eggs and slowly mix in the milk then beat until smooth.
3. Put the sausages in the air fryer basket, scatter over the sliced onion and drizzle over the oil. Roast for 12 minutes.
4. Remove from the air fryer, pour the batter over and around the sausages then return to the air fryer and cook for a further 32 minutes or until the sausages are cooked through and the batter is golden on top.
5. To make the gravy, heat a deep frying pan or saucepan and fry the remaining onion in the oil for 5 minutes until golden. Sprinkle over the flour and cook, stirring until thickened. Add the mustard, Worcestershire sauce and, gradually, the stock, stirring until smooth and thickened to your liking.
6. Serve the toad in the hole with the gravy to pour over.

Spicy Kale Chips

Prep time: 5 minutes | Cook time: 8 to 12 minutes | Serves 4

150 g kale, large stems removed and chopped
2 tsps. rapeseed oil
¼ tsp. smoked paprika

¼ tsp. salt
Cooking spray

1. Preheat the air fryer to 200ºC.
2. In a large bowl, toss the kale, rapeseed oil, smoked paprika, and salt.
3. Spray the air fryer basket with cooking spray, then place half the kale in the basket and air fry for 2 to 3 minutes.
4. Shake the basket and air fry for 2 to 3 more minutes, or until crispy. Repeat this process with the remaining kale.
5. Remove the kale and allow to cool on a wire rack for 3 to 5 minutes before serving.

Lush Snack Mix

Prep time: 10 minutes | Cook time: 10 minutes | Serves 10

170 g honey
3 tbsps. butter, melted
1 tsp. salt
180 g sesame sticks
230 g pumpkin seeds

200 g granola
150 g cashews
75 g crispy corn puff cereal
160 g mini pretzel crisps

1. In a bowl, combine the honey, butter, and salt.
2. In another bowl, mix the sesame sticks, pumpkin seeds, granola, cashews, corn puff cereal, and pretzel crisps.
3. Combine the contents of the two bowls.
4. Preheat the air fryer to 190ºC.
5. Put the mixture in the air fryer basket and air fry for 10 to 12 minutes to toast the snack mixture, shaking the basket frequently. Do this in two batches.
6. Put the snack mix on a cookie sheet and allow it to cool fully.
7. Serve immediately.

Baked Halloumi with Greek Salsa

Prep time: 15 minutes | Cook time: 6 minutes | Serves 4

Salsa:
1 small shallot, finely diced
3 garlic cloves, minced
2 tbsps. fresh lemon juice
2 tbsps. extra-virgin olive oil
1 tsp. freshly cracked black pepper
Pinch of salt
35 g finely diced English cucumber

1 plum tomato, deseeded and finely diced
2 tsps. chopped fresh parsley
1 tsp. snipped fresh dill
1 tsp. snipped fresh oregano
Cheese:
227 g Halloumi cheese, sliced into 1-cm thick pieces
1 tbsp. extra-virgin olive oil

1. Preheat the air fryer to 190ºC.
2. For the salsa: Combine the shallot, garlic, lemon juice, olive oil, pepper, and salt in a medium bowl. Add the cucumber, tomato, parsley, dill, and oregano. Toss gently to combine; set aside.
3. For the cheese: Place the cheese slices in a medium bowl. Drizzle with the olive oil. Toss gently to coat. Arrange the cheese in a single layer in the air fryer basket. Bake for 6 minutes.
4. Divide the cheese among four serving plates. Top with the salsa and serve immediately.

Crispy Jicama Fries

Prep time: 5 minutes | Cook time: 20 minutes | Serves 1

1 small jicama, peeled
¼ tsp. onion powder
¾ tsp. chili powder

¼ tsp. garlic powder
¼ tsp. ground black pepper

1. Preheat the air fryer to 180ºC.
2. To make the fries, cut the jicama into matchsticks of the desired thickness.
3. In a bowl, toss them with the onion powder, chili powder, garlic powder, and black pepper to coat. Transfer the fries into the air fryer basket.
4. Air fry for 20 minutes, giving the basket an occasional shake throughout the cooking process. The fries are ready when they are hot and golden.
5. Serve immediately.

Gammon, Egg and Chips

Prep time: <5 minutes | Cook time: 46 minutes | Serves 1

cooking spray
1 large baking potato, unpeeled, cut into chunky chips

1 tsp. olive oil
1 small gammon steak
1 egg

1. Preheat the air fryer to 200ºC and spay the air fryer basket with oil.
2. Drizzle the potatoes with the oil and some salt and pepper. Put in the basket for 22 minutes, until starting to go brown.
3. Remove and turn the chips.
4. Push to edges of the basket, put the gammon in the centre and cook for 7 minutes more. Set the chips aside and keep warm. Turn the gammon over, then crack the egg into the corner of the tray.
5. Cook for 7 minutes more until the egg is set and the gammon is cooked through.

Cheesy Jalapeño Poppers

Prep time: 5 minutes | Cook time: 25 minutes | Serves 6

2 slices bacon, halved
165 g whole milk ricotta cheese
120 g shredded sharp Cheddar cheese
1 spring onion, finely chopped

¼ tsp. salt
6 large jalapeños, halved lengthwise and deseeded
20 g finely crushed potato chips

1. Preheat the air fryer to 200ºC.
2. Lay bacon in single layer in basket. Air fry for 5 minutes, or until crisp. Remove bacon and place on paper towels to drain. When cool, finely chop.
3. Stir together ricotta, Cheddar, spring onion, bacon, and salt. Spoon into jalapeños; top with potato chips.
4. Place half the jalapeños in the basket and air fry for 8 minutes, or until tender. Repeat with the remaining jalapeños.
5. Serve immediately.

Onion Rings

Prep time: <5 minutes | Cook time: 10 minutes | Serves 12

cooking spray
120 g plain flour
½ tsp. sea salt

40 g cornflour
1 large onion, sliced into rings
100 ml sparkling water

1. Preheat the air fryer to 180ºC and spay the air fryer basket with oil.
2. Mix together 100 g of flour, cornflour, salt, pepper and sparkling water until smooth batter is achieved. Set aside until required.
3. Dip the onion rings into the leftover flour.
4. Tap to remove any excess, dip into batter and transfer into the air fryer basket.
5. Air fry for 3-4 minutes until golden and crispy.

British Stuffing

Prep time: 10 minutes | Cook time: 10 minutes | Serves 6

cooking spray
400 g breadcrumbs
200 g butter
1 medium to large onion

2 garlic cloves
5 tsps. dried sage
¼ tsp. salt and pepper

1. Preheat the air fryer to 180ºC and spay the air fryer basket with oil.
2. Chop the onion and garlic as finely as you can.
3. Add the butter, onion, dried sage and garlic to the basket and air fryer for 3 minutes.
4. Add the salt and pepper, stir then add the breadcrumbs little by little.
5. Transfer from the air fryer and stir until it is mixed well.

Crispy Prosciutto-Wrapped Asparagus

Prep time: 5 minutes | Cook time: 16 to 24 minutes | Serves 6

12 asparagus spears, woody ends trimmed
24 pieces thinly sliced prosciutto

Cooking spray

1. Preheat the air fryer to 180ºC.
2. Wrap each asparagus spear with 2 slices of prosciutto, then repeat this process with the remaining asparagus and prosciutto.
3. Spray the air fryer basket with cooking spray, then place 2 to 3 bundles in the basket and air fry for 4 minutes. Repeat this process with the remaining asparagus bundles.
4. Remove the bundles and allow to cool on a wire rack for 5 minutes before serving.

Roasted Aubergine Slices

Prep time: 5 minutes | Cook time: 15 minutes | Serves 1

1 large aubergine, sliced

2 tbsps. olive oil

¼ tsp. salt

½ tsp. garlic powder

1. Preheat the air fryer to 200ºC.
2. Apply the olive oil to the slices with a brush, coating both sides. Season each side with sprinklings of salt and garlic powder.
3. Put the slices in the air fryer and roast for 15 minutes.
4. Serve immediately.

Chapter 9 Desserts

Yule Log

Prep time: 20 minutes | Cook time: 18 minutes |
Serves 12 slices

cooking spray	**For the Icing:**
6 large eggs, separated	175 g dark chocolate,
150 g caster sugar	chopped
50 g cocoa powder	250 g icing sugar
1 tsp. vanilla extract	225 g soft butter
5 tsps. icing sugar (to	1 tbsp. vanilla extract
decorate)	

1. Preheat the air fryer to 180ºC and spay the air fryer basket with oil.
2. In a large, clean bowl whisk the egg whites until thick and peaking, then, still whisking, sprinkle in 50 g of the caster sugar and continue whisking until the whites are holding their peaks but not dry.
3. In another bowl, whisk the egg yolks and the remaining caster sugar until the mixture is moussy, pale and thick. Add the vanilla extract, sieve the cocoa powder over, then fold both in.
4. Folding in a dollop of egg white.
5. Then add the remaining whites in thirds, folding them in carefully to avoid losing the air.
6. Line a Swiss roll tin with baking parchment, leaving a generous overhang at the ends and sides, and folding the parchment into the corners to help the paper stay anchored.
7. Pour the cake mixture in the air fryer basket and bake for 18 minutes.
8. Let the cake cool a little before turning it out onto another piece of baking parchment.
9. Cover loosely with a clean tea towel.
10. To make the icing, melt the chocolate and let it cool.
11. Put the icing sugar into a processor and blitz to remove lumps, add the butter and process until smooth. Add the cooled, melted chocolate and the tablespoon of vanilla extract and pulse again to make a smooth icing.
12. Sit the flat chocolate cake on a large piece of baking parchment. Trim the edges of the Swiss roll.
13. Spread some of the icing thinly over the sponge, going right out to the edges. Start rolling from the long side facing you, taking care to get a tight roll from the beginning, and roll up to the other side.
14. Cut one or both ends slightly at a gentle angle, reserving the remnants, and place the Swiss roll on a board or long dish.
15. Spread the yule log with the remaining icing, covering the cut-off ends as well as any branches. Create a wood-like texture by marking along the length of the log with a skewer or somesuch, remembering to do wibbly circles, as in tree rings, on each end.

Apple Pie

Prep time: 30 minutes | Cook time: 20-22 minutes |
Serves 6

For the Pastry:	quartered
200 g plain flour	2 tbsps. freshly squeezed
1 pinch salt	lemon juice
110 g cubed unsalted	110 g sugar
butter	4 to 6 tbsps. cold water
2 to 3 tbsps. cold water	1 tsp. ground cinnamon,
For the Filling:	optional
700 g cooking apples,	25 g unsalted butter
peeled, cored, and	Milk, as needed for glaze

1. Place the flour, butter and salt into a large, clean bowl.
2. Rub the butter into the flour with your fingertips until the mixture resembles fine breadcrumbs, working as quickly as possible to prevent the dough becoming warm.
3. Add the water to the mixture and using a cold knife stir until the dough binds together, add more cold water a tsp. at a time if the mixture is too dry.
4. Wrap the dough in clingfilm and chill for a minimum of 15 minutes, up to 30 minutes. Preheat the air fryer to 220ºC.
5. For the Filling:
6. Simmer the apples with the lemon juice and water in a large pan until soft. Add the sugar and cinnamon to the cooked apples. Remove from the heat and add the butter and leave to cool.
7. Roll out half the pastry and line a 18-cm pie dish. Put the cooled, cooked apple mixture into the pastry case.
8. Roll out the remaining pastry to make a lid for the pie. Damp the edges of the pastry in the dish with a little cold water, cover with the lid, press the edges firmly together and crimp to decorate.
9. Brush the top of the pie with milk and bake in the air fryer for 20 to 22 minutes.

Banana and Walnut Cake

Prep time: 10 minutes | Cook time: 25 minutes | Serves 6

454 g bananas, mashed
227 g flour
170 g sugar
99 g walnuts, chopped
71 g butter, melted
2 eggs, lightly beaten
¼ tsp. baking soda

1. Preheat the air fryer to 180ºC.
2. In a bowl, combine the sugar, butter, egg, flour, and baking soda with a whisk. Stir in the bananas and walnuts.
3. Transfer the mixture to a greased baking dish. Put the dish in the air fryer and bake for 10 minutes.
4. Reduce the temperature to 166ºC and bake for another 15 minutes. Serve hot.

Victoria Sponge Cake

Prep time: 15 minutes | Cook time: 25 minutes | Serves 8

160 g unsalted butter, softened
160 g self-raising flour, sifted
160 g caster sugar
3 large eggs, lightly
beaten
1 tsp. vanilla extract
100 ml double cream
125 g strawberry jam
1 tbsp. icing sugar, for dusting

1. Preheat the air fryer to 150ºC. Grease and line a 20cm springform cake tins with nonstick baking paper.
2. In a large mixing bowl, cream together the butter, vanilla extract and sugar using an electric hand held whisk until light and fluffy.
3. Add the lightly beaten egg a tablespoon at a time, beating well between additions, until fully incorporated.
4. Carefully fold the flour in using a large metal spoon and spoon the batter evenly into the two prepared cake tins.
5. Bake for 25 minutes until springy to the touch and a cake tester comes out clean when inserted into the centre of the cakes.
6. Remove and allow the tins to cool on a wire rack for 5 minutes before turning out and peeling away the nonstick baking paper.
7. Whip the cream to soft peaks as the cakes cool, then spread the bottom half of the cake with the cream in an even layer.
8. Spread the strawberry jam evenly and carefully on top of the cream. Sandwich the cake with the other half of the cake and transfer it carefully to a serving plate. Dust with the icing sugar and serve.

Hearty Cheddar Biscuits

Prep time: 10 minutes | Cook time: 22 minutes | Makes 8 biscuits

290 g self-rising flour
2 tbsps. sugar
115 g butter. frozen for 15 minutes
120 g grated Cheddar cheese, plus more to
melt on top
320 ml buttermilk
125 g plain flour, for shaping
1 tbsp. butter, melted

1. Line a buttered 14-cm metal cake pan with parchment paper or a silicone liner.
2. Combine the flour and sugar in a large mixing bowl. Grate the butter into the flour. Add the grated cheese and stir to coat the cheese and butter with flour. Then add the buttermilk and stir just until you can no longer see streaks of flour. The dough should be quite wet.
3. Spread the plain (not self-rising) flour out on a small cookie sheet. With a spoon, scoop 8 evenly sized balls of dough into the flour, making sure they don't touch each other. With floured hands, coat each dough ball with flour and toss them gently from hand to hand to shake off any excess flour. Put each floured dough ball into the prepared pan, right up next to the other. This will help the biscuits rise, rather than spreading out.
4. Preheat the air fryer to 195ºC.
5. Transfer the cake pan to the basket of the air fryer. Let the ends of the aluminum foil sling hang across the cake pan before returning the basket to the air fryer.
6. Air fry for 20 minutes. Check the biscuits twice to make sure they are not getting too brown on top. If they are, re-arrange the aluminum foil strips to cover any brown parts. After 20 minutes, check the biscuits by inserting a toothpick into the centre of the biscuits. It should come out clean. If it needs a little more time, continue to air fry for two extra minutes. Brush the tops of the biscuits with some melted butter and sprinkle a little more grated cheese on top if desired. Pop the basket back into the air fryer for another 2 minutes.
7. Remove the cake pan from the air fryer. Let the biscuits cool for just a minute or two and then turn them out onto a plate and pull apart. Serve immediately.

Pineapple and Chocolate Cake

Prep time: 10 minutes | Cook time: 35 to 40 minutes | Serves 4

250 g flour
113 g butter, melted
50 g sugar
227 g pineapple, chopped
120 ml pineapple juice
28 g dark chocolate, grated
1 large egg
2 tbsps. skimmed milk

1. Preheat the air fryer to 190ºC.
2. Grease a cake tin with a little oil or butter.
3. In a bowl, combine the butter and flour to create a crumbly consistency.
4. Add the sugar, chopped pineapple, juice, and grated dark chocolate and mix well.
5. In a separate bowl, combine the egg and milk. Add this mixture to the flour mixture and stir well until a soft dough forms.
6. Pour the mixture into the cake tin and transfer to the air fryer.
7. Bake for 35 to 40 minutes.
8. Serve immediately.

Pear and Apple Crisp

Prep time: 10 minutes | Cook time: 20 minutes | Serves 6

227 g apples, cored and chopped
227 g pears, cored and chopped
125 g flour
200 g sugar
1 tbsp. butter
1 tsp. ground cinnamon
¼ tsp. ground cloves
1 tsp. vanilla extract
30 g chopped walnuts
Whipped cream, for serving

1. Preheat the air fryer to 170ºC.
2. Lightly grease a baking dish and place the apples and pears inside.
3. Combine the rest of the ingredients, minus the walnuts and the whipped cream, until a coarse, crumbly texture is achieved.
4. Pour the mixture over the fruits and spread it evenly. Top with the chopped walnuts.
5. Bake for 20 minutes or until the top turns golden brown.
6. Serve at room temperature with whipped cream.

Chocolate Coconut Brownies

Prep time: 15 minutes | Cook time: 15 minutes | Serves 8

120 ml coconut oil
57 g dark chocolate
200 g sugar
2½ tbsps. water
4 whisked eggs
¼ tsp. ground cinnamon
½ tsp. ground anise star
¼ tsp. coconut extract
½ tsp. vanilla extract
1 tbsp. honey
65 g flour
45 g desiccated coconut
Sugar, for dusting

1. Preheat the air fryer to 180ºC.
2. Melt the coconut oil and dark chocolate in the microwave.
3. Combine with the sugar, water, eggs, cinnamon, anise, coconut extract, vanilla, and honey in a large bowl.
4. Stir in the flour and desiccated coconut. Incorporate everything well.
5. Lightly grease a baking dish with butter. Transfer the mixture to the dish.
6. Put the dish in the air fryer and bake for 15 minutes.
7. Remove from the air fryer and allow to cool slightly.
8. Take care when taking it out of the baking dish. Slice it into squares.
9. Dust with sugar before serving.

Banbury Cakes

Prep time: 15 minutes | Cook time: 10-12 minutes | Serves 9 Banbury cakes

1 package ready made puff pastry
150 g currants
55 g unsalted butter
50 g mixed candied peel
½ tsp. cinnamon
½ tsp. nutmeg
110 g brown sugar
1 tbsp. port, sherry or rum
1 large egg white beaten
3 tbsps. caster sugar

1. Melt the butter and brown sugar, and add the dried fruit, spices, and port in a small saucepan. Let cool.
2. Preheat the air fryer to 220ºC and line the air fryer basket with oil. Roll out the pastry on a floured board ensuring a thickness of ½-1 cm.
3. Cut two lines across and 2 lines down to make 9 squares.
4. Place a tablespoon of the fruit filling in each square. Wet the edges of each square with water and bring the edges together to seal. Turn each bundle over, and shape it into an oval.
5. Dip each cake into the beaten egg and then dredge in the caster sugar. Place on the air fryer basket and make three diagonal cuts across each cake.
6. Bake for 10-12 minutes or until golden brown. Let cool before eating.

Chocolate Molten Cake

Prep time: 5 minutes | Cook time: 10 minutes | Serves 4

99 g butter, melted
3½ tbsps. sugar
99 g chocolate, melted

1½ tbsps. flour
2 eggs

1. Preheat the air fryer to 190ºC.
2. Grease four ramekins with a little butter.
3. Rigorously combine the eggs, butter, and sugar before stirring in the melted chocolate.
4. Slowly fold in the flour.
5. Spoon an equal amount of the mixture into each ramekin.
6. Put them in the air fryer and bake for 10 minutes
7. Put the ramekins upside-down on plates and let the cakes fall out. Serve hot.

Eccles Cake

Prep time: 10 minutes | Cook time: 12-15 minutes | Serves 8-12

cooking spray
500 g ready-made puff pastry
For The Filling:
75 g butter
150 g soft brown sugar
200 g currants

1 tsp. ground cinnamon
½ tsp. freshly grated nutmeg
grated rind of 1 orange
For The Glaze:
2 tbsps. milk
2 tbsps. demerara sugar

1. Preheat the air fryer to 220ºC and spay the air fryer basket with oil.
2. To make the filling, melt the butter and add all the rest of the ingredients and mix well. Leave to one side.
3. Roll the pastry to about 3 mm think and using a round cutter cut out circles, re-rolling the dough as necessary.
4. Place a teaspoonful of filling on to each circle.
5. Using a pastry brush, brush a little water all around the edge and fold one edge over to the other and seal well.
6. Turn it over so that the seal is underneath and roll carefully with the rolling-pin to flatten it into a round and place on the air fryer basket.
7. Make three slashes in the top of each with a sharp knife and brush lightly with milk and sprinkle with the demerara sugar.
8. Bake for 12-15 minutes or until golden brown.
9. Repeat the step 7 and 8 with all the other circles.

Yorkshire Parkin

Prep time: 15 minutes | Cook time: 45–60 minutes | Serves 16 squares

200 g butter, plus extra for greasing
1 large egg
4 tbsps. milk
200 g golden syrup
85 g treacle

85 g light soft brown sugar
100 g medium oatmeal
250 g self-raising flour
1 tbsp. ground ginger

1. Preheat the air fryer to 160ºC.
2. Butter a deep 22cm square cake tin and line with baking parchment. Beat the egg and milk together with a fork.
3. Gently melt the syrup, treacle, sugar and butter together in a large pan until the sugar has dissolved. Remove from the heat.
4. Mix together the oatmeal, flour and ginger and stir into the syrup mixture, followed by the egg and milk.
5. Pour the mixture into the tin and bake for 45–60 minutes until the cake feels firm and a little crusty on top. Cool in the tin then wrap in more parchment and foil.

Welsh Cakes

Prep time: <15 minutes | Cook time: 10 minutes | Serves 10 cakes

cooking spray
110 g salted butter, chilled, cut into cubes
225 g self-raising flour, sieved, plus extra for

dusting
85 g caster sugar
handful of sultanas
1 free-range egg, beaten

1. Rub the butter into the flour to make breadcrumbs. Add the sugar and sultanas, then stir in the egg. Mix, then form a ball of dough, using a splash of milk if needed.
2. Roll out the dough on a lightly floured surface until it is ½ cm thick. Cut it into rounds using a 7.5cm fluted cutter.
3. Preheat the air fryer to 200ºC and spay the air fryer basket with oil.
4. Place the Welsh cakes on the air fryer basket and bake for 2–3 minutes on each side, or until caramel brown.
5. Remove from the air fryer and dust with caster sugar while still warm.
6. Split them when cool and sandwich them together with jam.

Welsh Rarebit

Prep time: 10 minutes | Cook time: 10 minutes | Serves 6

cooking spray
350 g Mature Cheddar, grated
1 large egg, lightly beaten
2 tbsps. beer (preferably stout) or milk

1 tsp. Worcestershire sauce
1 tsp. English mustard
Pinch cayenne pepper
12 thick slices white bread

1. Set aside 1 heaped tablespoon of grated cheese.
2. Mix the rest with the egg, beer (preferably stout) or milk, Worcestershire sauce, mustard and cayenne.
3. Preheat the air fryer to 200ºC and spay the air fryer basket with oil.
4. Put the bread in the basket and bake for 4 minutes on both sides.
5. Spread the cheese mixture on top and then sprinkle on the reserved cheese.
6. Bake until the cheese is melted and starting to turn golden brown.

Ginger Snap Biscuits

Prep time: 15 minutes | Cook time: 12 minutes | Serves 16 biscuits

cooking spray
100 g self-raising flour
1 level tsp. bicarbonate of soda
2 tsps. ground ginger

40 g caster sugar
50 g unsalted butter, melted
2 tbsps. golden syrup

1. Preheat the air fryer to 170ºC and spay the air fryer basket with oil.
2. Sieve the flour, bicarbonate of soda and ginger into a bowl, then stir in the sugar.
3. Make a well in the centre of the dry ingredients and add the melted butter and the syrup. Stir until the mixture comes together to form a soft dough.
4. Divide the dough in half and cut each piece in 8. Roll each portion into a ball.
5. Place 8 balls on the air fryer basket, then flatten slightly. Bake for 12 minutes until golden and cracked on top. Leave to firm up on the basket for 10 minutes, then transfer to a wire rack to cool completely.
6. Repeat step 5 with the remaining biscuits.

Cinnamon and Pecan Pie

Prep time: 10 minutes | Cook time: 25 minutes | Serves 4

1 pie dough
½ tsp. cinnamon
¾ tsp. vanilla extract
2 eggs
180 g maple syrup

⅛ tsp. nutmeg
3 tbsps. melted butter, divided
2 tbsps. sugar
75 g chopped pecans

1. Preheat the air fryer to 190ºC.
2. In a small bowl, coat the pecans in 1 tbsp. of melted butter.
3. Transfer the pecans to the air fryer and air fry for about 10 minutes.
4. Put the pie dough in a greased pie pan and add the pecans on top.
5. In a bowl, mix the rest of the ingredients. Pour this over the pecans.
6. Put the pan in the air fryer and bake for 25 minutes.
7. Serve immediately.

Simple Pineapple Sticks

Prep time: 5 minutes | Cook time: 10 minutes | Serves 4

½ fresh pineapple, cut into sticks

22 g desiccated coconut

1. Preheat the air fryer to 200ºC.
2. Coat the pineapple sticks in the desiccated coconut and put each one in the air fryer basket.
3. Air fry for 10 minutes.
4. Serve immediately

Fried Golden Bananas

Prep time: 5 minutes | Cook time: 7 minutes | Serves 6

1 large egg
30 g cornflour
30 g plain bread crumbs

3 bananas, halved crosswise
Cooking oil
Chocolate sauce, for drizzling

1. Preheat the air fryer to 180ºC.
2. In a small bowl, beat the egg. In another bowl, place the cornflour. Put the bread crumbs in a third bowl.
3. Dip the bananas in the cornflour, then the egg, and then the bread crumbs.
4. Spray the air fryer basket with cooking oil.
5. Put the bananas in the basket and spray them with cooking oil. Air fry for 5 minutes.
6. Open the air fryer and flip the bananas. Air fry for an additional 2 minutes.
7. Transfer the bananas to plates. Drizzle the chocolate sauce over the bananas, and serve.

Sticky Toffee Pudding

Prep time: 15 minutes | Cook time: 40-45 minutes | Serves 8

cooking spray
175 g self raising flour
1 tsp. baking powder
75 g butter, room temperature
150 g light muscovado sugar
2 Eggs, beaten
175 g dates, roughly chopped

80 g chopped walnuts
150 ml hot water
Toffee Sauce:
125 g butter
175 g light muscovado sugar
170 ml cream
80 g chopped walnuts

1. Preheat the air fryer to 180ºC and spay the air fryer basket with oil.
2. Lightly grease and base line a 18 cm square tin. Put chopped dates into a bowl and pour over the hot water.
3. Place flour, baking powder, butter, sugar and eggs into a large bowl and beat until smooth.
4. Add the dates, water and chopped walnuts and stir until well blended.
5. Transfer to prepared tin and bake for 40-45 minutes until well risen, nicely browned and springy to the touch. Turn onto a wire tray to cool.
6. Meanwhile, make sauce by putting all ingredients into a saucepan over a low heat and gently stirring until butter is melted, sugar is dissolved and sauce has thickened slightly. Do not boil, just allow to simmer.
7. Cut the pudding into 8 squares, place on serving plate and spoon over the toffee sauce.

Yorkshire Pudding

Prep time: 20 minutes | Cook time: 25 minutes | Serves 6

100 g plain flour
¼ tsp. salt
3 large free-range eggs

225 ml milk
4 tbsps. sunflower oil

1. Preheat the air fryer to 220ºC.
2. Mix the flour and salt together in a bowl and make a well in the centre. Add the eggs and a little milk.
3. Whisk until smooth, then gradually add the remaining milk.
4. Pour the mixture into a jug.
5. Measure a tsp. of oil into each hole of a 12-bun tray.
6. Transfer to the air fryer basket and bake for 5 minutes, or until the oil is piping hot.
7. Carefully remove from the air fryer and pour the batter equally between the holes or the tin. Return the batter quickly to the air fryer and cook for 20 minutes, or until golden brown and well-risen. Serve immediately.

Apple and Walnut Muffins

Prep time: 15 minutes | Cook time: 10 minutes | Makes 8 muffins

125 g flour
70 g sugar
1 tsp. baking powder
¼ tsp. baking soda
¼ tsp. salt
1 tsp. cinnamon
¼ tsp. ginger
¼ tsp. nutmeg

1 egg
2 tbsps. pancake syrup, plus 2 teaspoons
2 tbsps. melted butter, plus 2 teaspoons
190 g unsweetened applesauce
½ tsp. vanilla extract
30 g chopped walnuts
45 g diced apple

1. Preheat the air fryer to 165ºC.
2. In a large bowl, stir together the flour, sugar, baking powder, baking soda, salt, cinnamon, ginger, and nutmeg.
3. In a small bowl, beat egg until frothy. Add syrup, butter, applesauce, and vanilla and mix well.
4. Pour egg mixture into dry ingredients and stir just until moistened.
5. Gently stir in nuts and diced apple.
6. Divide batter among 8 parchment-paper-lined muffin cups.
7. Put 4 muffin cups in air fryer basket and bake for 10 minutes.
8. Repeat with remaining 4 muffins or until toothpick inserted in centre comes out clean.
9. Serve warm.

Conclusion

The above-shared classic British Air Fryer recipes are perfect for creating a diverse and extensive menu for all the routine meals and special celebrations. If you have a quality air fryer at home, then it's about time to put it to the best use. A multifunctional Air Fryer with medium-large capacity has the most utility as it is best for home use. This cookbook highlights all the features of this kitchen miracle and shares an extensive menu that can be created using nothing but an Air Fryer. Give all of its amazing and flavoursome recipes a try and enjoy the ultimate dose of next-level crispiness. Once cooked, you can easily reheat the food in the same appliance. An Air Fryer is all about ensuring convenience for all the foodies and home chefs. And this cookbook is here to help you cook like professionals with minimum effort and maximum ease.

Appendix 1: Measurement Conversion Chart

WEIGHT EQUIVALENTS

METRIC	US STANDARD	US STANDARD (OUNCES)
15 g	1 tablespoon	1/2 ounce
30 g	1/8 cup	1 ounce
60 g	1/4 cup	2 ounces
115 g	1/2 cup	4 ounces
170 g	3/4 cup	6 ounces
225 g	1 cup	8 ounces
450 g	2 cups	16 ounces
900 g	4 cups	2 pounds

VOLUME EQUIVALENTS

METRIC	US STANDARD	US STANDARD (OUNCES)
15 ml	1 tablespoon	1/2 fl.oz.
30 ml	2 tablespoons	1 fl.oz.
60 ml	1/4 cup	2 fl.oz.
125 ml	1/2 cup	4 fl.oz.
180 ml	3/4 cup	6 fl.oz.
250 ml	1 cup	8 fl.oz.
500 ml	2 cups	16 fl.oz.
1000 ml	4 cups	1 quart

TEMPERATURES EQUIVALENTS

CELSIUS (C)	FAHRENHEIT (F) (APPROXIMATE)
120 °C	250 °F
135 °C	275 °F
150 °C	300 °F
160 °C	325 °F
175 °C	350 °F
190 °C	375 °F
205 °C	400 °F
220 °C	425 °F
230 °C	450 °F
245°C	475 °F
260 °C	500 °F

LENGTH EQUIVALENTS

METRIC	IMPERIAL
3 mm	1/8 inch
6 mm	1/4 inch
1 cm	1/2 inch
2.5 cm	1 inch
3 cm	1 1/4 inches
5 cm	2 inches
10 cm	4 inches
15 cm	6 inches
20 cm	8 inches

Appendix 2: Air Fryer Time Table

Vegetable

Item	Temp(°F)	Time (mins)	Item	Temp(°F)	Time (mins)
Asparagus (sliced 2-cm)	205°C	5	Mushrooms (sliced ½-cm)	205°C	5
Aubergine (4-cm cubes)	205°C	15	Onions (pearl)	205°C	10
Beetroots (whole)	205°C	40	Parsnips (1-cm chunks)	195°C	15
Broccoli (florets)	205°C	6	Peppers (2-cm chunks)	205°C	15
Brussels Sprouts (halved)	195°C	15	Potatoes (small baby, 650 g)	205°C	14
Carrots (sliced 1-cm)	195°C	15	Potatoes (2-cm chunks)	205°C	12
Cauliflower (florets)	205°C	12	Potatoes (baked whole)	205°C	40
Corn on the cob	200°C	6	Runner Beans	205°C	5
Courgette (1-cm sticks)	205°C	12	Sweet Potato (baked)	195°C	30 to 35
Fennel (quartered)	190°C	15	Tomatoes (cherry)	205°C	4
Kale leaves	120°C	12	Tomatoes (halves)	180°C	10

Chicken

Item	Temp(°F)	Time (mins)	Item	Temp(°F)	Time (mins)
Breasts, bone in (550 g)	190°C	24	Legs, bone in (800 g)	195°C	30
Breasts, boneless (150 g)	195°C	14	Wings (900 g)	205°C	12
Drumsticks (1.1 kg)	190°C	20	Game Hen (halved – 900 g)	200°C	20
Thighs, bone in (900 g)	195°C	22	Whole Chicken (3 kg)	185°C	75
Thighs, boneless (700 g)	195°C	20	Tenders	185°C	8 to 10

Beef

Item	Temp(°F)	Time (mins)	Item	Temp(°F)	Time (mins)
Burger (120 g)	190°C	16 to 20	Meatballs (7-cm)	195°C	10
Filet Mignon (250 g)	205°C	18-20	Ribeye, bone in (2-cm, 250 g)	205°C	12 to 15
Flank Steak (700 g)	205°C	13	Sirloin steaks (2-cm, 350 g)	205°C	10 to 14
London Broil (900 g)	205°C	20 to 28	Beef Eye Round Roast (1.8 kg)	200°C	45 to 55
Meatballs (2-cm)	195°C	7			

Pork and Lamb

Item	Temp(°F)	Time (mins)	Item	Temp(°F)	Time (mins)
Loin (900 g)	185°C	55	Bacon (thick cut)	205°C	6 to 10
Pork Chops, bone in (2-cm, 200 g)	205°C	13	Sausages	195°C	15
Tenderloin (450 g)	190°C	15	Lamb Loin Chops (2-cm thick)	205°C	8 to 12
Bacon (regular)	205°C	5 to 7	Rack of lamb (600-1000 g)	195°C	23

Fish and Seafood

Item	Temp(°F)	Time (mins)	Item	Temp(°F)	Time (mins)
Calamari (250 g)	205°C	5	Tuna steak	205°C	7 to 10
Fish Fillet (2-cm, 250 g)	205°C	12	Scallops	205°C	5 to 7
Salmon, fillet (200 g)	195°C	12-14	Prawn	205°C	5
Swordfish steak	205°C	10			

Frozen Foods

Item	Temp(°F)	Time (mins)	Item	Temp(°F)	Time (mins)
Onion Rings (350 g)	205°C	9	Fish Sticks (300 g)	205°C	11
Thin Chips (550 g)	205°C	13	Fish Fillets (1-cm, 300 g)	205°C	15
Thick Chips (500 g)	205°C	20	Chicken Nuggets (350 g)	205°C	10
Mozzarella Sticks (300 g)	205°C	8	Breaded Prawn	205°C	9
Pot Stickers (300 g)	205°C	8			

Appendix 3: Recipes Index

Reference

https://www.shutterstock.com/zh/image-photo/avocado-egg-sandwiches-coffee-healthy-breakfast-1937557699

https://www.shutterstock.com/zh/image-photo/homemade-baked-mexican-chips-nachos-nonfried-174906881

https://www.shutterstock.com/zh/image-photo/homemade-breaded-fried-avocado-fries-chipotle-396103177

https://www.shutterstock.com/zh/image-photo/chickpeas-cookies-sugar-free-gluten-chocolate-2058902921

https://www.shutterstock.com/zh/image-photo/deep-fried-sundried-pork-moo-dad-1851022999

https://www.shutterstock.com/zh/image-photo/omelet-fried-mushrooms-fresh-herbs-plate-2173347029

https://www.shutterstock.com/zh/image-photo/grilled-cheese-tomato-sandwich-on-white-1261971322

https://www.shutterstock.com/zh/image-photo/fried-sliced-zucchini-served-yogurt-dip-2187474471

https://www.shutterstock.com/zh/image-photo/lemon-semolina-crusted-fish-fries-green-160896395

https://www.shutterstock.com/zh/image-photo/sirloin-steak-on-plate-296732015

https://www.shutterstock.com/zh/image-photo/baked-mustard-honey-chicken-breasts-cherry-1420269884

https://www.shutterstock.com/zh/image-photo/sumpia-mini-crunchy-spring-rolls-on-2225542217

https://www.shutterstock.com/zh/image-photo/traditional-christmas-fruit-mince-pies-on-2228344333

https://www.shutterstock.com/zh/image-photo/delicious-fast-easy-asparagus-tarte-made-2181383559

https://cn.depositphotos.com/380997866/stock-photo-deep-fried-seafood-shrimps-squid.html

https://cn.depositphotos.com/31586019/stock-photo-fried-organic-coconut-shrimp.html

https://www.freepik.com/free-vector/closeup-on-appetizing-hot-pizza-pepperoni-withsalami_8913317.html

https://www.freepik.com/free-photo/crispy-fried-chicken-plate-with-salad-carrot_6632395.htm

https://www.freepik.com/premium-photo/chicken-schnitzel-with-sauce-fried-potatoes-lemon-plate_30487653.htm

https://www.freepik.com/premium-photo/raw-skewers-meat_15532633.htm

https://www.freepik.com/premium-photo/deep-fried-chicken-wing-with-garlic-sauce-korean-style-serve-with-kimchi-pickled-radish-wooden-table-asian-food-concept_16112317.htm

https://www.freepik.com/premium-photo/female-hands-cuts-piece-cake-with-butter-cream-decorated-with-summer-strawberries-blueberries_15415136.htm

https://www.freepik.com/premium-photo/fried-chicken-with-french-fries-nuggets-meal_5864795.htm

https://www.freepik.com/premium-photo/fried-chinese-spring-rolls-served-with-chili-sauce-decorated-rose-tomatoes-with-green-leaved-wood-space-concept-asian-food_6050465.htm

https://www.freepik.com/premium-photo/prawn-tempura_1332616.htm

https://www.freepik.com/free-photo/roasted-whole-chicken-with-christmas-decoration_18922724.htm

https://www.freepik.com/premium-photo/steak-beef-beef-steak-medium-with-red-pepper-aromatic-herbs-fried-onion_6731450.htm

Printed in Great Britain
by Amazon

16655268R00045